Life happens

Violeta Stavrositu   Cristi Stavrositu

Life happens

Bucharest

National Library of Romania
Life happens, Stavrositu Violeta, Stavrositu Cristi
Copyright © 2023, Bucharest, paperback edition,
All rights reserved.

ISBN 978-973-0-38929-6

Originally published as "Viața se întâmplă", in 2022,
in Bucharest, Romania, paperback edition
Copyright© 2022, Stavrositu Violeta, Stavrositu Cristi
ISBN 978-973-0-36509-2 All rights reserved.

Cover design by Violeta Stavrositu
Cover illustration by Kelly Stevens - Mc.Laughlan
Trust's photo, page 243, by Gabi Pisla

lifehappensbook@gmail.com
instagram: our.stories.in.books
phone: +40 758 549 589

Contents

"To let go of control
     and follow the natural stream of life,
     is to gain control for the first time."

~ Vigdis Garbarek

Foreword

The title of the book refers to the fact that life happens within a moment, and the moment is new, surprising and unknown to anyone, because no one can know something that has not happened yet. Please note that this book is not recommended to famous fortune tellers.

But the fact that we don't know what the next moment will be like should not prevent us from hoping and planning, on the contrary, it should make us aware that we can and must do only our part. And that's all.

Life manifests itself spontaneously, always new, beyond any words and concepts, and according to natural principles, as very well **Leonardo da Vinci** observed hundreds of years ago when he said:

"Nature never breaks its own laws".

When we are able to look at life with fresh eyes, everything makes sense and thus **everyday life becomes sacred**, as in fact it always has been, only that sometimes our eyes can no longer see it.

Cupid

They were at one of the lunches that they were having together with all their fellow participants. Cristi, who *happened to be sitting* across from Violeta, was trying to start a conversation with her, but she kept looking out the window, fixedly in the opposite direction. After a few moments, Cristi curiously asked her:

'What are you looking at?'

'At a Dalmatian, you very rarely see Dalmatians', she replies.

'Rarely indeed... I also have a dog at home, it's a puppy...'

'Do you have a dog? What kind?'

'Labrador.'

At that moment, Violeta was prevented from uttering a single word by a sudden, sharp pain in her foot. The lady sitting next to her was trying to catch her attention by digging her high heel into Violeta's foot.

The owner of the pointed shoe was a good friend of hers, who overhearing the conversation, discreetly wanted to make her attentive, knowing how much Violeta loves Labradors. She loved them so much that every time she saw one in the street she had to go and stroke him. She has always stopped to do so, even when she was driving!

When Violeta heard about the existence of a Labrador in Cristi's life, she became so happy that she forgot about the pain in her foot. She would have loved to see him right away, but as the puppy was in Bucharest, she was content to ask him if he had any photos. Cristi was on the lookout and instead of showing her a photo, he asked for her email address so he could send her the puppy's photos.

Violeta, curious and impatient to see the puppy, gave Cristi the address. It was a *checkmate to the queen*.

The scene had taken place in an Italian restaurant, during one of the breaks of the neurolinguistic programming course by Kutschera Institute, where they first met. They did not think then how important they would soon become to each other, nor did they know how life in its mysterious and surprising ways had brought them together from hundreds of miles away. And they certainly had no idea of the magical part of the story, when life in its ingenious way introduced a Labrador into the scene who played the part of Cupid with great skill.

Many emails followed with the most adorable Labrador Violeta had ever seen and who was just a peerless seven-month-old puppy at that time. Ever since she was a little girl, Violeta had been in love with Labradors. She had seen in movies that in the happy families there was always a Labrador. It was even present in the pictures on the mantelpiece. As a child, she thought that a Labrador was the condition of a joyful family, so she hoped that one day she would have one too…

And the expression "had it never happened, it wouldn't be told" fits perfect here, because if it wasn't for the Labrador in question, this true story wouldn't be either.

**Life is so ingenious,
that can even use a Labrador as Cupid.**

Trust

At first the Labrador puppy was nameless and yet he was complete and perfect as he was.

Over time, however, he received all kinds of names from those who played with him, and then he had to have a name of his own. Cristi named him Trust and it turned out to be the most suitable name for this loyal and honest English Labrador, who you could always count on.

His big, black, deep and bright eyes revealed a sparkling presence of spirit which animates a gentle, loving, playful and friendly yellow Lab, foodie and very funny.

If we were to listen to what people said, Trust was a very beautiful Labrador, such a rare specimen, as we were often told. But since we don't really follow gossip, we can say without exaggeration that there never was and never will be another one like him. According to the writer W. R. Pursche: "every man thinks he has the best dog. And they all are right."

Trust played impeccably many roles but primarily the role of Cupid who made this true story exist. He was also the best companion because one could count on his calm presence regardless of the circumstances.

Trust's calmness was not conditioned by the hustle and bustle around him.

Trust's calmness was based on the fact that he felt good in his coat and he lived according to his own nature.

His mission began early in the morning: Trust was the cutest alarm clock. He waited quietly near the bed until he knew we were awake. Then he would put his muzzle on the pillow and look at us happily, wagging his tail. The wet nose, like a huge black truffle in front of our eyes, woke us up, telling how much he missed us. It's impossible not to have a beautiful morning, when the first being you see shows you how lovable you are. It was a living proof that every day is an important day and deserves to be lived as beautifully as possible.

Next came his role as the most persistent sports coach, because there was not a morning in which he did not invite us to a session of gymnastics exercises on the floor. After that, of course, there was a walk in the fresh morning air, which usually also included cardio exercises: running unexpectedly after a cat. Although the cats always won the race, Trust never gave up. Surely he was also their coach, because otherwise we can't explain the reason why he was running after them. He didn't want to catch them anyway.

When it happened that the cat was not in the mood to run and stayed put, Trust would greet her with a glance and go on his way. If the cat ruffled her hair and arched her back as if to scare him and drive him away, Trust slowly and curiously approached to smell the athlete. The harder the cat curled up to look fiercer, the more intrigued Trust became and he approached to sniff her better. If the cat ran away, so did Trust — even taking us along if we had him on a leash. When the cat stopped, he stopped too. A movie-like chase scene was created between the two characters, a scene that, most of the time, attracted amused spectators, who took pictures or filmed the two protagonists. It was a full-on comedy show.

Once the morning run was over, Trust was very careful to remind us that it was time for a delicious breakfast.

We can wake up joyfully every morning.
The fact that we are alive is a reason enough!

Every day we can find out something new.
There are so many things we can discover.

Trust in Austria

The Black Panther

It was our first winter holiday together and Trust's first time using his passport. We chose Austria, because we knew it is a spectacular, civilised country, rich in culture and tasty food. In addition, we were pleasantly surprised by the way the pets were treated. We remembered the words of Mahatma Gandhi: " **The greatness of a nation and its moral progress can be measured by the way animals are treated.**"

We could go into almost every store with Trust, although he wasn't really interested in buying anything but Viennese schnitzels.

In restaurants, when a waiter came to the table to take our order, he immediately brought Trust a bowl of water and asked us if they could bring him something to eat. The fact that you feel so welcome with your furry friend makes you even more careful not to disturb anyone, to keep him close to you in crowded places and of course to leave the place clean.

Our first stop was Vienna, which we explored and admired for several days, far and wide. Trust had just turned a year old, he was full of energy and curiosity to discover new places, smells and of course delicious flavours.

We were staying at a hotel with a more avant-garde design, which in the reception area had a life-size black panther statue, so much bigger than a Labrador. The statue was so well made that when we saw it for the first time we were amazed. Trust was intrigued by the Black Panther from the beginning. He would give it a short bark every time we came in or out, a sort of *Good morning* or *Good evening*, after which, as the Panther was rude and did not return his greeting, Trust would come a little closer, go around it, and because the Panther would stand still, he would get even closer and subject it to the ultimate dog test: smelling.

But in the case of the Black Panther, the lack of smell confused Trust even more, for he no longer understood how this large, silent, black creature could not even have a smell. It was truly an unprecedented and extraordinary oddity.

Trust could understand that the Black Panther had not been educated and therefore did not answer his greeting, but he did not lose hope and continued to greet it every time we were there. Of course he could also understand that maybe the Black Panther was too tired or too lazy to move, because he also was some-times tired after running or swimming for hours, and then all he wanted to do was sit into a cool corner where he could quietly snore to his heart's content. But what he didn't under-stand at all was how one could be so bad-tempered as not to even wag the tail, if still standing, that is, not sleeping?

That was too much for Trust!

And the biggest enigma was why the mysterious creature had no smell? It went against everything Trust knew. The interaction between Trust and the Black Panther was so funny that every time it caused laughter among the customers, hotel staff and those who happened to be around at the time.

After that ritual which took place at least twice a day, that is when we were going out and when we returned, we went on our way, in which, it is true, we didn't meet black panthers anymore, but almost every time we met dogs willing to play, sniff and measure themselves with Trust. Or to wag their tails. And if the dogs we met didn't do so, at least they barked. And most importantly for Trust, to smell, so that he could recognise them, that is, he could at least estimate who he was dealing with, unlike the rude Black Panther.

**The fact that someone is grumpy,
has nothing to do with you.**

Trust the dancer

One of the beautiful days spent in the imperial and enchanting city of Vienna, we parked the car on a street with imposing buildings full of history and set off to explore the area. Vienna is such a vibrant and fascinating city, with a rich architecture from baroque to modern, with buildings from different centuries blending amazingly in a harmonious way, that it has something for everyone.

We also arrived at one of the most visited addresses, the place where Sigmund Freud, the "father of psychoanalysis", lived most of his life, practised and laid the foundations of discipline. The building now hosts the Freud Museum and the largest psychoanalytic library in Europe. The place impregnated with memories, takes you back in time. You feel like you've entered Freud's universe. The letters received from Einstein are proof that those interested in knowledge have always found ways to communicate. The pictures on the walls show his love for Jofi, his ChowChow dog, who accompanied him to therapy sessions. It is said that Freud noticed the calming effect of patients in Jofi's presence and took her opinion into account for their evaluation. If Jofi approached, it meant the patient was calm, if Jofi moved away, he knew the patient was tense. At the time, however, the world was skeptical of a dog's ability to smell people's emotional states and to soothe simply by her calm, loving presence. Only after a few decades, after a lot of clinical studies and research, it was concluded that Freud's intuition had been accurate and the foundations for the Animal Assisted Therapy were beginning to be laid, with extraordinary health benefits and impressive results in treating depression, post traumatic stress and other conditions.

Of course, after that foray into time, we treated ourselves with an aromatic coffee in Café Freud, a pleasant place with a welcoming decor that invited you into a moment of reflection.

Because Trust was patient and understanding with us, when we got back to where we had parked the car, we thought it would be good to honour him with a football game before we left. We started playing with the ball on the sidewalk. Until then Trust's ball game was very simple, the ball was kicked and he, being a retriever, would run after it and bring it back to us.

This time, however, when I wanted to shoot, Trust positioned himself in front of the ball like a real goalkeeper and stood so alert that I effectively had nowhere to pass the ball. Then I suddenly changed the position I was in, trying to make him think I was going to shoot with my right foot, but the next moment I changed my foot to trick him, only he was so on the ball that he kept switching legs with increasing speed. Suddenly, I realised that we were dancing like we were in a mirror. It was so funny to see Trust dancing on that beautiful winter evening in Vienna. The classical music that could be heard from one of the houses made the whole scene magical.

We would probably have stayed there for a long time because we were feeling so good, plus we were bringing smiles to the faces of those who passed by, but we noticed that a large sheet of paper was taped to the driver's side window of our car. As large and efficiently attached as it was, it didn't seem like a good sign.

Our debutante dancer looked very surprised when we abruptly stopped the performance and went to check what it was all about. Instead of charging something for our impromptu show, we found out by reading the paper that we had to pay a parking fine. We told ourselves that we would pay it the next day and consider it as rent for the stage on which the Trust performance took place, but when we got into the car we saw that we also had a huge yellow wheel clamp. So we called them and waited for the unlockers. They weren't late, but before they came we took advantage of the rented stage and the music that was still playing in the background and did another dance to Trust's great delight. So the fine was worth all the money, because the show was complete, including a welcome encore.

Who would have imagined that Trust would dance for the first time on a *stage* in Vienna?

Life really does bring amazing moments
that have to be fully enjoyed,
just as a dog relishes a bone.

Enigma from Salzburg

Our next stop on the way to the ski resorts was beautiful Salzburg, the city of Mozart. We really wanted to see this wonderful city, with its impressive architecture, culture and beautiful surroundings at the foot of the Alps.

Walking and admiring each place full of history we understood why a large part of the old centre of Salzburg is a UNESCO World Heritage Site.

It really is a charming, neat and cheerful city. A city that conveys that **the people who live in it, love it and want to live there.**

Baroque style and modern art blend perfectly, making it a city suitable for all ages. You have so many options that no matter how long you stay, there will always be something to visit.

Shop windows were adorned with Mozart-kugeln, chocolate pralines boxes of all shapes and sizes, with Mozart's image on them. They looked so attractive and inviting! In most of the shops and restaurants, Mozart's music could be heard softly. A real delight.

We also saw the oldest restaurant in Europe, believed to have been opened in 803 and still operating, and the place where Mozart often dined.

Still admiring and contemplating, and Trust still exploring, we reached the beautiful area called the Horse Fountain and immediately after, we saw the tunnel that connects the old town to one of the districts of Salzburg: the Sigmundstor tunnel, the oldest tunnel in Austria, 430 feet long. Curious that he had not been in a pedestrian tunnel before, he picked up speed. At some point, we didn't see him anymore, so we also stepped up. As we took a few steps into the tunnel, we saw Trust speeding back with something very large in his mouth, partially wrapped.

We tried to see what it was and we were surprised when we realised it was a whole ham on the bone, cooked and steaming!

It was such a sight to see Trust coming out of the tunnel with that huge steaming *jamón* ham in his mouth. We couldn't believe it, we were looking at each other, looking in all directions to see if we were on hidden camera. How can your dog come out of the tunnel with that huge ham in his mouth?

It felt surreal. We looked around to see who gave it to him, but we didn't see anyone nor a store. We were totally surprised and Trust was very cautious lest we should take his *jamón* ham. We waited for a while to see if someone came from the tunnel or if the people from the hidden camera came to tell us it was a prank. No one came, so it would forever remain a mystery to us.

Trust was eager to eat it, eyeing a suitable spot for the wonder dinner. He found a safer place, sat down and started to enjoy it, and we were watching him and our mouths were watering. It smelled so good and the vapours lifted the scent right up to our noses.

We were eagerly waiting for him to finish his Salzburg feast so we could go to a restaurant too. When Trust finished eating the big and tasty ham, we also went to get something to eat. Our dinner was very good, but it smelled nowhere near like Trust's dinner.

Austria may not be the country where "dogs walk with pretzels on their tails", but it is certainly the country where you can meet a happy dog with a whole ham on the bone in his mouth, on the street. A steaming ham on a frosty winter day, that miraculously appeared in Trust's mouth and whose provenance will remain an enigma to us.

Life really is surprising! It's good to go through life with your eyes wide open, or if you're a Labrador with your nose sniffing in the wind, because you never know what's just around the corner.

Life happens,
let yourself be surprised,
even spoiled sometimes.

Trust the Chieftain

We had just returned from the mountains to our cosy and welcoming flat in the beautiful ski resort of Bad Gastein. We had spent the whole day in the mountains, and now it was so nice to sit in the warmth and amuse ourselves with the day's adventures. Because when you have a Labrador with you it is almost impossible to avoid adventures.

That day we had taken the gondola lift up to the top of the ridge. It was very funny how

Trust waited for a gondola to arrive and when its doors opened, he inspected it, smelled it and let it pass. Then he waited for the next gondola and did the same, to the amusement of everybody who watched him. About the third or fourth gondola, he went up and we followed. We thought it was safe because it had been checked by Trust.

From the gondola, Trust looked curiously at how the snow-covered fir trees looked from top to bottom. Every now and then another gondola came down from the other direction, and Trust watched it until it was out of sight, as if to make sure it got down safely. To him, the gondolas were like giant red balls, bouncing merrily up and down.

Up in the mountains the scenery was charming, all immaculate white, bright sun, and time seemed to stand still. Trust was always fascinated when he arrived at a new place and tried to discover it as well as he could. And as it was full of snow there — his favourite after seawater — Trust was in seventh heaven. So were we. We definitely would have stayed there all day if we hadn't been hungry.

We went down next to the ski slopes in a single file, through the generous layer of fluffy snow. Trust was our trusted *chieftain* leaping like a deer and we were jumping in the deep tracks he left. From time to time he would stop and check that his tribe was complete. At one of the stops, to our surprise, we saw that the tribe had increased considerably. It seemed we weren't the only ones in need of food.

One of the newcomers began to sing yodellers — songs specific to the inhabitants of the Alps — and the rest of us, slowly and timidly at first, joined in. Without realising it, we were vocalising together, each in his own language, as if we were good friends on an expedition. Trust was the only one not singing, because he had to be careful where he was leading us. He had a lot of responsibility considering we were up on the ridge.

The journey to the place where the inviting smells were coming from was a real delight for all the tourists. We said goodbye and Trust was petted and congratulated for having guided us safely and on the shortest route. No wonder, with his strong sense of smell, especially for food.

We left Trust on the sunny terrace and entered the restaurant where the steaming food was so inviting. We grabbed trays and helped ourselves with their specialties, making sure to put something good also for Trust, who had certainly detected the aroma of food fresh off the fire.

All the dishes looked so appetising that everyone would have liked to taste everything. Austrian gastronomy is famous for being savoury, which is why Austria is also called the land of flavours. And to be able to eat food like that in the middle of the mountains after a few hours spent in the snow, was something down-right fantastic.

We were at the cash register, dizzy with the aromas from the plates, but the moment we wanted to pay, we were told that it was not possible by card. Then we noticed how instinc-tively our hands clutched the trays, in a way that made it clear that we weren't going to give up our chosen goodies so easily, especially since Trust was waiting outside hungry and ravenous, so we simply couldn't return without our *prey*. If we had to do the washing up or clean the floors, so be it …

The lady immediately understood and asked us serenely:

'Are you still skiing here tomorrow?'

'Yes, we're going up for sure!' we answered in chorus.

'Okay, then you'll pay tomorrow.'

We breathed a sigh of relief hearing such good news. She wrote the amount on a piece of paper and pinned it to the wall behind her. We then saw several notes stuck on the wall, clearly there were others like us. So we went out on the terrace triumphantly and enjoyed the goodies with Trust, warmed by the sun's rays and admiring the splendid view.

Thus we had a great day in the mountains, but let's get back to when we returned to the flat.

As we sat relaxing and talking, at one point we realised we hadn't seen Trust in a while. He usually sat at our feet or very close, watching us until he fell asleep. We looked around through the flat but we didn't see Trust; we asked ourselves whether we opened the front door and both of us said no. The thick layer of snow on the terrace was intact, obviously Trust had not gone out.

It felt bizarre. We looked around the apartment once more. No trace of Trust. We look under the bed, under the sofa, under the armchairs...nothing. One could think that there was a secret exit like in the adventures of Arsène Lupin.

We went around the whole flat, called him, and looked again on the terrace, in the hall, in the bathroom, kitchen and bedroom. No sign of Trust. We were about to sit in the living room to catch our breath, when we saw him, on the armchair with his back to us, fast asleep! He had taken the round shape of the armchair, and as it was golden like his fur, it was completely camouflaged.

We understood then how much our beliefs can deceive us, how they influence our perception, so that instead of seeing the reality, we see what we think it is, based on the past, based on the known. In our minds, if Trust had been there, he could only be on the floor, never perched in an armchair, because Trust never climbed onto beds or armchairs. Besides, we had called him, so we were sure he couldn't be there, because he used to come immediately when we called him.

But the mind hadn't taken into account that after a day in the snow Trust would be sound asleep and even though he was close, he couldn't hear us.

It was a very good moment of reflection on how we humans **react most of the time, based on habit, instead of looking with fresh eyes at what is in front of us.**

The next day we took the cable car and went up the mountain again to pay for our meal and of course we enjoyed something else, because warm Austrian dishes are so good after a long walk in the snow.

Look at the world with fresh eyes.
Life is new every moment.

Trust at ski

All Labradors are eager to accompany people wherever they go and participate in all the activities they do. That's how they are. If in some cases that was a great advantage, such as relaxing the atmosphere at a business meeting, regarding skiing we had to find a good solution for everyone. The problem wasn't that Trust couldn't keep up with us, not at all, he was running in the snow at a speed that was hard to match, but with other skiers on the slope we couldn't let him go.

We were lucky to be on the slopes with a group of friends, so Trust took turns keeping company for those taking a break. He stood at our meeting place and kept looking curiously up the slope, as if he was a watchful and dedicated coach for his team, waiting impatiently for his skiers.

Only the stopwatch was missing.

At one point, believing that the one coming down was a skier from his team who was in trouble and couldn't stop at the meeting place, Trust rushed after him. Seeing that, we went after Trust, but with ski boots on our feet, not only did we fail to catch him, but we no longer saw him after a short while, so quickly had he gone down, or rather, so slowly were we moving. We immediately turned around, put on our skis and sped off after him, but as we turned the first curve, we could see Trust coming back determinedly towards us. We didn't know if he had caught up with that skier or his sense of smell told him that the skier did not belong to our team, but he was surely coming back and was resolute to regain his place in the middle of the team.

It was such an experience to venture into the Alps with Trust. He loved the snow and the company of people so much that it was a real delight to have him around. Our friends who were on a ski slope with a Labrador for the first time, were simply fascinated by his cheerful presence.

And as it was a pity to be in the Kaprun area and not admire the entire region from the "Top of Salzburg" panoramic platform, we decided to climb the glacier as well at almost 10,000 feet altitude. Some of the group wanted to retreat to the warmth to eat something good, and Trust, who had an immediate under-standing when it came to food, showed his intention to go with them. We decided to meet again in the après-ski at the base of the slope.

It was truly spectacular and well worth it. Coming down, we felt grateful to those who over the years had worked so hard to make these splendid places so accessible.

Eager to get to the meeting place, we opened the door and were surprised by the great party atmosphere inside. We were astonished to suddenly enter such a party, from the silence of the mountain.

Everyone in the bar had gathered in a circle, dancing exuberantly. It seemed to be a dance in which the one in the middle is imitated by those forming the circle. We tried to see who had the leading role. You could tell that he was a dancer appreciated by those around him, but as the dance floor was completely full, it was quite difficult to move forward. One thing was certain, everyone was having great fun.

When we got closer and could see inside the circle, we couldn't believe it: the one dancing in the middle of it was no ordinary dancer, it was …Trust!

Raised on two legs, he passed from one to the other, flapping his paws as if in a well-known dance. The whole bar rejoiced in the atmosphere that had been created. We were speechless, beaming with joy, surprise and gratitude.

We retired to our friends' table without Trust seeing us, to let him continue his fun. We looked at him happily and as if we couldn't believe what a day we had lived. Trust had brought so much joy to the people on the slopes, and now he was cheering up so many people he was seeing for the first time.

As someone once said "only a dog can go to a party, talk to no one, wipe out food, fall asleep under the table, and still be the most popular guest."

Life simply happens. That's what it does! In the morning when we went skiing, we had no idea that we were going to live a truly fabulous day.

Stepping out the comfort and the known zone, we have a chance to get to know ourselves. Only by knowing ourselves can we live fully.

Always enjoy seeing a loved one,
even if the last time was only a few minutes ago.
You never know when it's the last time.

Trust and the Archaeologist

A funny story

We had recently moved on a street that ended with a lake, a beautiful and quiet area of Bucharest at that time. We were still discovering the neighbourhood, the right places for walking with Trust, the dogs and the cats living there.

On that day it was just me, Violeta, out for a short walk with Trust, when a man who seemed to know us said hello in a friendly manner. He petted Trust and talked very nicely to him. I assumed he was a neighbour who probably had met Trust before, when he was with Cristi. Looking at Trust, he told me very proudly:

'I also had two, today!'

Because he was staring at Trust when he said that, I understood that he was referring to two dogs. The fact that he spoke of them in the past, immediately worried me that he might have abandoned them. Frightened I asked him:

'And… What did you do with them?'

'I buried them!'

'But…were they dead?' I was shocked by what I had just heard.

'Dead?! Of course they were dead!' he answered, annoyed by my question.

I didn't have the courage to ask more, for fear of finding out something even more up-setting. I immediately said goodbye and hur-ried home.

I didn't know what to think, I was really shocked by his direct and unrepentant way in which he talked about burying two dogs. I was kind of sorry I didn't ask him how they died and if they had been old or sick. But at the same time I was glad I didn't learn more distressing details about something that had already hap-pened anyway and there was nothing I could do about it. But I was intrigued by the fact that they were both buried at the same time. Anyway, it was something very strange.

After a few days, we met him again and that time, I was with Cristi. He greeted us joyfully, although he looked tired, his clothes were a bit dusty, and he had a shovel in his hand.
We returned the greeting, and he continued to tell us very proudly:

'I have had one today, too. I have resolved it!'

Confused, we looked at each other and suddenly realising the comic of the situation, we asked him:

'Do you work at the graveyard?'

'Yes! I am the archaeologist.'

'The archaeologist?'

'Yes, I mean the gravedigger.'

'Does this mean that the other day when we talked, it wasn't about dogs?'

'Oh gosh, you thought I buried dogs?! I couldn't bury a dog, I love dogs so much!'
Our talk and the situation were downright hilarious, even though it was on such a serious subject.

It was also a confirmation of the fact that **every man speaks of his own reality.**

Trust wagged his tail the moment we laughed, whether he understood what we were talking about or not, we couldn't tell. The Archaeologist assumed that Trust was happy to see him, and that made him happier. And since laughter and good humour are *contagious*, a few passers-by also *got infected*. We parted amused and cheerful, for you cannot be less cheerful than the gravedigger.

🐾 🐾 🐾 🐾

When we were living there we came across the Archaeologist several times, each time we were thoroughly amused and amazed. He was always joyful and grateful for little things, things that we humans generally appreciate when we no longer have them. Many times, we live with the illusion that everything belongs to us.

The fact that he was so often in contact with death,
made him appreciate Life so much!

Trust
the Elephant King

It was a frosty winter day and as it had snowed all night, our usually quiet street was utterly frozen, as if overnight it had turned into a fairy tale landscape.

Trust, who had just woken up, looked out the window amazed by such beauty. He couldn't believe it. Everything was silvery-white, pure and shining.

We were all eager to get out, although we knew the walk would be shorter because it was very cold indeed. I mean it was cold for us, for Trust it was perfect because he had real fur that we couldn't match no matter how thickly we dressed. And no matter how much we loved snow, we couldn't love it as much as he did. Because Trust really loved snow like only a Labrador can. Or maybe a Saint Bernard.

After a short walk, we headed home, but Trust showed his intention to stay outside the house as he still had to check on some snow drifts that had appeared overnight and which he had just discovered. He was so cheerful to play in the snow that he would have stayed out all day if he hadn't gotten hungry. It reminded us of our childhood days, when we played all day long in the snow without getting cold or hungry.

We didn't see any danger in leaving him outside, as there wasn't a single person in the street, and cars were out of the question because there was so much snow that the street was completely blocked. Back then, we often used to leave him alone outside in front of the house, where he would explore freely for a few minutes, then come to the gate and enter.

We were trying to strike a balance between keeping him on a leash and letting him loose when we thought it was safe, so that he too could feel that he was fully alive.

If the gate was closed he only barked once. He had an unmistakable baritone bark, which he used very rarely, only when he really had something important to convey and had no other means of making himself understood, such as when he found the gate closed.

Trust always barked one brief woof and then waited for us to open the gate. No one had taught him that, but we imagined he didn't want to be taken for the postman. Because, as you know from the bestselling book or the famous movie,"The Postman Always Rings Twice."

It was delightful to see him wait with his big black eyes on the entrance door. He was so focused that even a black cat could have passed behind him without being chased.

That day, however, more time passed and Trust didn't return. We looked out of the windows in the two directions he could have gone, we didn't see him so we got dressed again and went out after him. We barely got to the gate and called him, when we saw the Archaeologist, cheerful as usual and with a tricksy look.

'Are you looking for the dog?' he asked us out of the blue.

'Yes! Have you seen him?'

'Yeah sure!' he replied proudly.

'Where did he go?' we asked.

'Come with me!' he invited us, waggishly.

'Is he hurt? Where is he?' we asked scared.

'He's not hurt, calm down!' he said jovially, crossing the street and inviting us to follow him.

We tried to follow him through the snow-drifts, when suddenly he disappeared through the gate of the small graveyard across the road. After a moment of hesitation, we also got in. We saw him walking very determinedly towards one side, and we followed him. At one point we reached a very small house with black smoke coming out of the chimney. We were both very surprised when we saw the inhabited house, because we did not know that people who are alive *live* in the graveyard.

The Archaeologist opened the door and invited us into his little house. From the doorway we looked suspiciously inside, and what we saw was something completely unexpected: Trust was sitting relaxed on a turquoise trunk with golden locks, as if it was taken from an oriental tale. Pillows of various sizes and patterns were underneath and around him. He was covered in something silky and colourful like a rainbow. Perched on that fairy tale trunk in the small room, Trust looked huge.

He looked just like the Elephant King in full regalia, and the trunk beneath him was like a throne. As oriental as everything looked, we expected the smoke in the room to come from incense sticks with exotic flavours, but no, the smoke arose from an old cast iron stove. When he managed to see us through the smoke, the Elephant King began wagging his tail gladly. It was as if the parade had begun, and we were the first participants. His expressive face said:

How do you like my surprise?
The same could be read on the Archaeologist's cheerful and satisfied face, which conveyed that their prank had succeeded.

Having reassured ourselves that Trust really had not suffered anything, on the contrary, he had been raised to the rank of the Elephant King of the hospitable palace in the land of the righteous, we asked the troublemaker how he had come up with such a crazy idea. He just waited to be asked, and as enthusiastic as a child told us:

'Today I have a day off, because the ground is frozen, so I went out for a walk in the neighbourhood. I met Trust in the street. He also seemed frozen, so I took him with me to warm him up. He immediately followed me, I think he was curious to see where I live. I invited him inside, right on the trunk, because it's warmer up there, and I covered him with a blanket that I got as a gift from a lady and that I keep for the holidays. But what better celebration than Trust's visit? Trust is my best friend, he wags his tail every time he sees me, even when we meet several times a day. He's always joyful as if we haven't seen each other for a long time. And I had never given him anything, not even a bone. I just wanted to give him something. So I got him warm, put more wood on the fire, and sat by the stove, but I thought you might be looking for him, and I came to tell you. I was right, you were looking for him, wasn't it lucky that I came to tell you?'

We couldn't say anything. Can you be mad at Trust's friend when his intention was to warm him up and spend time together? You can't, so instead of getting upset, you feel like you want to reward him. We asked him to come to our place to give him something too, but he told us:

'Don't worry, it is my gain for having the best company!'

It filled our hearts with joy to realise that Trust was able to bring so much good cheer to a man living alone in a graveyard on a frosty winter day when there was nobody on the streets. We re-membered the expression: "sometimes, a helping hand can even come in the form of a paw."

When we got home we invited Trust straight into the shower stall and with the best smelling shampoos and shower gels, we got the smoke out of his fur. After the snow bath, the smoke bath and the scented foam bath, the Elephant King fell fast asleep, to complete the successful ceremony.

As Trust's friend put it: "it had been a very good day!"

**Sometimes when you feel lonely,
you can find company in a furry friend.**

The best day

Together with a neighbour, we had planted a few young oak trees in front of the house, hoping that when they grow, their rich crowns will provide a welcoming shade during the hot days in Bucharest, and will be a good host for the birds. We had bought one more tree to plant by the lake where we often walked with Trust, next to a bench that was not very usable in the summer as it had no shade at all.

So one Saturday when we wanted to plant it, we thought of Trust's friend the Archaeologist, who besides being always kind and willing to help, also had a spade. He came at once and lifted the oak with enthusiasm and ease, and put it on his shoulder, although it was twice his height. When we got to the car, we told him we were going to put the back seat down, put the oak diagonally, and the trunk of the SUV would remain open.

'Where is Trust to sit? ?' he wondered.

'Trust will be waiting for us at home', we answered.

'Oh no, by no means. Trust will sit on the back seats with me, and I will hold the tree out of the window!'

'Out of the window?? It's too heavy!!'

'Too heavy an oak tree?!'

Seeing him very determined and confident, we took him at his word. He got into the back seat, put his arm out of the window, and we let him hold the young tree trunk by its middle.

Intrigued by what was going on, Trust jumped into the car, quickly climbing over the Archaeologist as if to help him keep his balance. What we saw in the side mirrors resembled a scene from a play: on the right side of the car, an arm holding the tree was hanging out, with the Archaeologist's cheery face above; on the left side window a large yellow Labrador head appeared with the ears blown back, with big curious eyes enquiring about our destination, and a pink tongue hanging out in an attempt to cool down — it was a hot day and he had been fidgeting around us, lest he should be left out.

We quickly got to the chosen place and before we knew it, our experienced Archaeologist had already dug the hole, with Trust's participation of course, who although was not good at digging, was proving supportive and helpful by pushing aside the dug ground with his big paws. Everything happened so fast, that before the oak realised what was happening, its roots were already enjoying the nourishment of the freshly watered ground. That was how the oak tree had a place of its own, where it could grow strong roots and mirror itself in the clear water of the lake.

We watered the oak tree for a few weeks, but Trust took this activity very seriously and *watered* it every time we passed by, for years on end.

He stopped at it, smelled it curiously, marked it every time and surely remembered the wonderful experience of planting the tree.

On the way back, the Archaeologist's face was beaming with joy and he confessed to us that that day was the best day. We looked at each other and wondered if he really was serious, because we had only asked him to help us plant a tree, not to join us at a party. As if he sensed our confusion and wanted to clarify, he added:

'This morning I went to the market and bought some vegetables, with which your next door lady neighbour is making me a delicious soup as we speak.. Then I got my job done for today and I was glad you called me; you drove me around, we planted an oak tree and I also received a good tip, and the icing on the cake is that I spent so much time with Trust who even kissed me! What more can I wish for?!'

We understood that he was very serious, and the honest way in which he shared his joy was like a reminder that life is made of little things that we so often ignore.

These so-called little things are actually very important. When we see them with fresh eyes and do them wholeheartedly, we live a life in which we feel fulfilled.

At any age, we can start again to see the extraordinary in everyday life.

The Love between Labradors and the sea
is eternal Love.

Trust's Seaside Adventures

Trust and the Sea

When we were at the seaside, Trust's favourite strategy was to drop the ball at the feet of people standing on the beach. He would look them straight in the eye, wagging his tail, and when he caught someone's eye, he would direct it to the ball. There were few who resisted him and refrained from throwing the ball and getting into his game. Almost every time he found a play partner. And they quickly became friends, because Trust was friendly and reliable.

Everything was straightforward for him, he played until he was tired or hungry, and the game ended with Trust walking home with the ball in his mouth, leaving his playing partner smiling, cheerful and fascinated that he had played with such a big dog, a dog he didn't even know, but in whose presence he felt so safe. It is an absolutely wonderful experience to play with a Labrador on the beach. **And because he was so gentle and trustworthy, many people got rid of their fear of dogs playing with Trust.** He always played very fair, according to strict rules, rules that he himself had designed. Trust never deviated from those rules. If he dropped the ball at somebody's feet, it meant it was their turn and he would wait until they played. He also had a way of nodding his head, from top to bottom, by which he communicated that he was ready, and it was your turn.

When the ball was thrown into the sea, he swam and brought it back to the shore. He never passed the ball while he was still in the water, only on the sand. His partner was supposed to wait until Trust put it down, not try to get it out of his mouth, he wouldn't have succeeded anyway. Trust used to leave the ball for the next throw at the feet of somebody he chose. Sometimes he would choose someone else, for reasons known only by himself, and the one he had been playing with would be out of the game for that round, meaning that would sit and watch from the touchline. Trust kind of knew who needed a bit of invigoration. People were amused and amazed at his tenacity.

You could have complete confidence that he would never jump at the ball in your hand. He used to wait patiently and ran only after the ball was thrown. And because he strictly followed the rules, he was completely trustworthy. He fully deserved his name, Trust.

Many times in the evening, when we took Trust for a walk on the beach, we would hear people saying: "This is the Labrador we played with earlier today." We have heard those words many times. And some, more daring, came to us, petted his head and asked us what his name was and whether he would come to the beach the following day. Trust was the attraction and the joy of beaches wherever we went. One of the funniest questions we have often been asked was:

'How did you teach him to swim?'

'We didn't unteach him!' we puzzled them in return.

In whatever country we were, Trust always found friends to play with, regardless of nationality or language. His sense went beyond the limits of language, because he used a simple language that anyone could understand, namely **the universal language of love**.

And because it was impossible to resist the invitation to be joyful, meetings with Trust were always authentic experiences, and authentic experiences remain with us forever. A special bond was quickly created with Trust. We were very used to being asked first about him and then about us.

Some people became so attached to Trust that year after year they came from the other end of the resort to see Trust and spend a few hours with him. Some parents told us that when they asked their children in which resort they wanted to go to the sea, the children answered indignantly: 'what do you mean where? At Trust!.' For them, it was as if the sea and Trust were part and parcel, they could not be separated. The children hoped that Trust would be at the sea all summer long, because Trust loves the sea. And because we loved both the sea and Trust, in the summer we used to move and work there. And the love was mutual, not only did Trust love the sea, but the sea also loved Trust, because he played with it the most. And that's why the sea called him year after year, and we couldn't resist the call either...

Between Trust and the sea, it was love at first sight. Trust-puppy, when he first reached the beach and felt the fine sand under his paws, he was so joyful that he began running, as he was trying to find an end to the sea, to embrace it all with his paws. He stopped only after a few miles, tired but content.

His expressive face seemed to say: *I'm so glad I found you, I want to be together with you for the rest of my life.* And so it was, because the love between Labradors and the sea is eternal.

If it was off-season and he couldn't find anyone to play with, Trust played with the waves of the sea. He noticed that if he dropped the ball from his mouth, the sea would steal it from him, but he would retrieve it on the next wave. It was so beautiful to watch how patiently he waited for the ball and how well he knew when to grab it. And then he would let it go again and wait. It was still his favourite game except that when he played it with the sea, the game was reversed: the sea became Trust's retriever. And when the sea got rough, because the sea is not always calm and predictable like Trust, then he would jump in and swim to retrieve his ball, and he would do so, because he was a retriever all the time, unlike the sea, which only became a retriever sometimes when playing with Trust.

At night, when the beach was deserted the sea felt lonely, and missed Trust. To lure him, the sea would bring a ball which had been stolen the other day and put it on the shore. The sea knew Trust would be her first guest, after the seagulls, but the seagulls never came for the balls, the sea was waiting for them with shells.

**If you want to have real friends,
be a good friend, to yourself and to other.**

Trust in love

A beautiful summer evening, we were taking a walk with Trust on the beach. Fascinated by the beauty of the sky reflected in the warm sea water and relaxed by the unmistakable smell of the breeze, at one point we realised that we were walking the dog without a dog. That is, Trust was no longer with us. In a place well known to him, we used to unleash him, and he was walking around us curiously sniffing what was new or interesting.

We called him, looked for him, but Trust was nowhere. A few friends saw us looking for him and immediately joined us. We all called Trust, whistled to him, but nothing. No sign of the Labrador. We went to look for him even further, although he wouldn't leave us unless he really had an important reason, because yes, Labradors sometimes have important *missions*. And when he had a mission, he was unstoppable.

That's how we understood that Trust walked with us on a leash just for our sake, and that if he wanted to run, he ran with the leash too. Trust was very strong, because he had been swimming all summer.

But let's go back to the summer evening when a whole bunch of people were looking for him, in vain. Even though we couldn't see it in those moments of concern, there was a beautiful side to the situation: so many people were coming together at once, united for the sake of Trust and motivated by a common desire to find him.

It was already getting late, we were all

exhausted, so we stopped the search and retreated hoping that he would return on his own when he finished the *mission* he had left us for. And we were hoping that someone would call us after seeing the phone number on the collar. That was what we used to do when we met unaccompanied dogs with collars around their necks. It was like a modern version of Radio Holiday, where in the old times it was announced which children were found on the beach, so that way they could be recovered.

Exhausted, we had just fallen asleep when suddenly the phone rang. It was the most joyful awakening and the best news to hear that Trust was well. The man from the guard company called us. When he heard that we couldn't find Trust, he had alerted all the guards in the area through his walkie-talkie. One of his colleagues, from the other end of the resort, had informed him that he had just seen a yellow Labrador with a purple medallion on his neck, accompanied by a young female dog, at the newly opened Greek restaurant.

Apparently Trust had invited the *girl* to a late dinner. Or, who knows, maybe he had been the one invited. We couldn't be upset because we knew how much Trust loves Greek food. Who does not like it?

It was so romantic to hear that our young adventurer took the *girl* out to a restaurant. Obviously he was very much in love with her, otherwise the gourmand Trust would not have shared any of the food. Especially Greek food.

Joyfully, we suddenly forgot the scare we had been through and went at once to retrieve *the inamorato*. And that was how we found out that a Greek restaurant opened near us, and that brought a smile to our faces. The next evening we got our revenge, leaving him at home to wait for us, while we went out for a romantic dinner, at the restaurant recommended by Trust and his one summer love.

Be yourself,
no matter how others want you to be.

Mr. Trust

A few weeks after the romantic Greek dinner, we were still at the seaside, where Trust enjoyed great daily swimming time. He would plunge in after the ball was thrown as far as possible into the sea, caught it and swam with it in his mouth straight to the shore, where he would gladly return it to the thrower. Bringing the balls back was his main activity, because Trust is a retriever who always returns what he receives. Even love, but not food!

Trust always kept the food warm and safe. Labradors are said to be so much in love with food and want to take great care of it, so they store it in their tummy like in a safe.

So Trust was in great shape: he swam a lot, ate well, slept well, played as much as he wanted. In short, he enjoyed a content life. But one day, the call of love spoke its word and the tranquillity turned into an unstoppable run.

The *girl* he had taken out to the Greek restaurant at the beginning of the season had now gone into heat. Trust suddenly turned into a male, and not an ordinary male, but a very determined one.

On that hot day there followed the most terrible race through the entire resort, because other suitors were competing for the attractive *girl*. From the sea to the lake, from the lake back to the sea crossing the road, which was a real danger. All   attempts to catch him were in vain. The competition was fierce and the *Cup* was too important for Trust to give up. Six other dogs, some with collars and some without, including a Husky who growled at Trust every time they met, followed *the girl*, each hoping that he would be the lucky winner.

A friend of ours, a strong Transylvanian guy and on top of that a *forever Metallica fan*, offered his help to catch Trust. In such a serious company, we set out very confident that we would catch Trust quickly. Our optimism was high, but what we didn't anticipate at the time is that the force driving Trust on the *girl's* trail **is the greatest force in the universe, the force of Love.**

Seeing that seven suitors had gathered behind her, the young female dog ran off faster than one could imagine. After nearly an hour of running, interrupted by brief stops, during which we saw Trust trying to do with the young female dog something he had never done before, the dogs reached a strip of land that ended in the lake. They had nowhere to run, they had to turn around, and that was our chance.

We stood at an equal distance one from the other, to cover as best we could the only place through which they could turn back. They had stopped and were watching us. It was confrontation time.

The girl dog looked to see which of us was the weak link and scurried right through us at high speed. Immediately Trust also approached in speed and at that moment our friend flung himself spectacularly to catch him. The determination with which our Transylvanian rocker sprang was over-whelming. There was no way that Trust could escape. His plunge reminded us of Duckadam* from that memorable night when he was called "the Hero of Seville."

And yet... miraculously, Trust managed to slip through his fingers and... "Goooal!". We couldn't believe it. Trust was able to move on. Anyway, the plunge was incredible!

Unfortunately we didn't have time to enjoy it, because our players were back on the field running super fast towards the road.

---

* Helmut Duckadam is a Romanian retired footballer who played as a goalkeeper. He was dubbed "the Hero of Seville" due to his performance in the 1986 European Cup Final, won by his club Steaua București, where he saved all four penalties against Barcelona in the penalty shootout, for the first time in football history.

In a hurry, we also crossed the road, trying to stop the passing cars, by using signs. Miraculously, none of the eight dogs were hit although the road was very crowded being in peak season.

We breathed with relief when we saw that the dogs had all crossed safely and were heading towards the sea. We were already exhausted after an hour of continuous running in the summer heat.

They were getting ahead of us, and at some point we could no longer see them.

When we reached the sea they were nowhere to be seen. We went back another way and tried to sniff out their trail. Suddenly we stopped and could not believe the scene we were seeing in front of our eyes: in the garden of the most famous restaurant nearby, Trust's first love story was taking place! And not anyway, but with spectators: the six male dogs who had admitted defeat in front of him. This is the story of how he became Mr. Trust.

Then we understood why we had not been able to catch him: that experience had to happen. He had to win *the cup of love.*

The girl did not forget that Trust had courted her, walked with her all over the resort, spent so many evenings together by the sea and took her to the best Greek restaurant, so she finally gave him her love.

She wasn't running away from him — Trust told us — but from the other dogs!

A few months later, we also received a puppy from the lady who was taking care of the girl dog — as it is customary — the male gets a puppy, the others stay with the female.

We named him Junior and gave him up for adoption to a man whose wife and dog had recently died.

Junior has gentle eyes like Trust's, his fur has a similar colour, but he is smaller in size. With a beautiful character, Junior is quiet, curious and loving. Although we've never had him tested for paternity, we love him and believe he is Trust's pup for sure.

And as life never ceases to surprise us, in the first pictures received from his new companion, Junior had a scarf from a famous football team around his neck, and the gentleman was happy to report that they enjoyed watching football matches together and were the greatest supporters.

**Life has its surprising way,
and Love always knows the way!**

In the so-called little things,
a truly good life is hidden.

City Boy Trust

Trust an artiste

To express his joy, Trust gave a performance almost every day. Those were the moments that he became so funny. It was impossible not to stop what we were doing and watch it, especially since we knew it only lasted a few minutes. It would have been a shame to miss out on a good laugh.

The more we had fun, the more intense and funnier his show became. He was doing all kinds of acrobatics which you didn't expect to see from a dog his size, plus he wasn't exactly skinny. And he did them rhythmically and with astonishing speed. Sometimes he would quickly catch a toy or an object in his mouth and these became his props for that show. Seeing that his performance was appreciated, he also offered us an encore. And Labradors, like people, enjoy it when they feel appreciated.

The fact that he saw us full of joy and that we were saying "well done Trust" had a huge impact on him. He enjoyed it even more than when we rewarded him with a treat, although Labradors are known to have a good appetite.

His performances were different each time — just like **life which is always new, never repeating itself** — but they had something in common, each time they happened spontaneously.

The time or place of the performance was never announced, and each show would only begin if it had at least one spectator. He never played if the hall was empty.

It seemed that Trust totally agreed with Einstein on how to live your life, because he lived as if everything was a miracle.

"There are only two ways to live your life.
One is as though nothing is a miracle.
The other is as though everything is a miracle."

~ Albert Einstein

You won't believe it but Trust could make people laugh even when he was asleep. Once, on a summer evening we were having dinner with several friends, at a restaurant. Cristi was sitting at the head of a long table, the atmosphere was relaxed when suddenly we saw a little boy running towards us and shouting:"Tati! Tati!"*

We looked behind us but there was no one else. We were curious to see who the little boy called "tati" (daddy).

The child resolutely walked towards Cristi, who looked surprised. All eyes turned inquiringly towards Cristi and then even more so to Violeta. The child had already approached Cristi, with open arms, he seemed to know him very well!!

————

* "Daddy! Daddy!"

We all were taken aback, and waited for Cristi's reaction. He didn't get to make any gesture because the child bent down and got under the chair...where Trust was sleeping!

We realised then, that the little boy was actually calling out Trusty — the way we lovingly called Trust — but being very young, he couldn't pronounce the r's and s's yet, so instead of Trusty he said ...Tati (Daddy).

We all calmed down, especially since the real "tati"(daddy) appeared in the meantime. He was a business partner of ours and therefore the child knew Trust, but we ourselves saw the child for the first time.

Trust woke up, stared at us and didn't understand why we were all looking at him and laughing heartily. He was used to people laughing when he performed, but not out of the blue. Trust went back to sleep after the little boy left, not knowing what he had stirred around him.

It is better not to rush to make assumptions, as some things are not what they appear.

Trust the walker

One of the hidden blessings of living with a furry companion is the need for daily walks in all seasons. When the weather is fine, walking is a delight. But what do we do when the weather is harsh? Then it becomes very challenging. Since we don't like what we should do, we will put up some resistance and try to trick life.

At one point in our life, we even had a neighbour who in winter would walk down to the front door of the building, open it a little, just enough to let her Fox Terrier out, while she stayed inside holding onto the retractable leash. It was a kind of tele-guided ride, by cable at that time, because the wireless version had not yet been invented. We believe that the Fox Terrier was convinced that in winter, because it is cold, the earth contracts so much that it ends up being only ten square yards. Nothing more!

But what our young neighbour didn't know is that precisely in going beyond the comfort zone, a blessing is hidden. Only when we manage to overcome our habit of resisting to what is new, and the desire to just sit in the warmth, do we begin to feel that we are truly alive and fully enjoying what life offers us, even when the conditions seem unfavourable. The fact that we manage to face any weather makes us stronger. Over the years spent with Trust we have noticed a very interesting thing: our immunity has considerably strengthened and we have hardly ever caught a cold.

If truth be told, sometimes when the weather is extremely cold and piercing we don't really feel like walking. But for Trust, with his thick Labrador coat, there is no such thing as a cold day, for him every day is just a good day to go for a walk.

So when he was asking to go out, we optimistically told ourselves, let's just take him out for as long as he needs and we'll immediately lure him back with a reward. But just as the expectation seldom matches the reality, our attempt to fool Trust was doomed to failure. When he saw himself outside, his senses were awakened and he wanted to keep sniffing. We were already frozen so we tried to bring him back, but he knew he barely got out. We wanted to lure him back in, but he understood immediately and did not get hooked on our bait. He took no notice of our plan. Then we convinced ourselves that if we went on a little further, just up to the first corner, he too would want to turn back realising he was the only dog out in such sharp weather.

But for Trust it was a world full of smells and each smell conveyed some new and important messages. Sometimes those messages could also be urgent. He was so focused and diligent in deciphering fresh information that we grew curious too. He stopped and sniffed every area as if he was reading an email. Read out loud, the emails would have probably sounded something like this: *hmm...so that dog from another district came again. Aha...and a new girl dog appeared in the area; let me see who else was here last night? Yes, yes, another stranger...and also my playmates.... but where are they now? What? Was I so late that I missed the morning meeting? What's wrong with these people, they get scared of a little cold, one can hardly take them out for a refreshing walk!*

After each stop, we hoped that that was really the last one, that maybe he got tired of deciphering so many messages, or he even finished his research. Unfortunately the frost had dulled the scents and the exploration kept on. When by our estimation the walk was over, we wanted to return home. But not him. He pulled back and looked at us as if to say without words: hey, did you forget the route?! Don't you understand that we have to meet at least one dog and that socialising is important even in winter?!

We didn't have the heart to say no, and

although our hands, feet, and faces were numb with cold, we went on in the penetrating dampness, while our minds dreamt of a warm and sunny place. Suddenly, as if to wake us up from dreaming, Trust disappeared. We looked for him, but could not see him through the thick fog spreading from the lake. We called him, but to no avail. We weren't scared, because there were no cars by the lakeside and besides, Trust knew the area well. After a few minutes, the phone rang, from an unknown number. Surprise!

We were invited by the lady who lived in the villa by the lake to join Trust in her living room and have a hot coffee together. She knew us from our daily walks past her house with Trust. When she was walking through the gate with her Bichon, Trust followed them wanting to play with the little dog. But due to her Bichon not liking the cold, they quickly entered the house.

She used the phone number written on Trust's collar to call us. The lady seemed pleased that her Bichon was playing with Trust, because she said her dog wasn't usually very playful. We were glad to know that Trust inspired playfulness in the fragile white doggy. Again Trust looked like Gulliver in Lilliput.

We all laughed at how Trust, smelling our intention to take him home quickly, managed to trick us, leaving us outside in the cold while he played inside, in a warm cosy place.

It was very nice to see once again how thanks to Trust we meet wonderful people, people with whom we share the same values and with whom we have become real friends.

**Every day can be a good opportunity
to get out and enjoy the fresh air
when you have a furry friend.**

Trust loves tennis balls

One of Trust's favourite activities when we lived near some tennis courts was to go and *pick up* a ball. We went daily as if we had season tickets. We would leave our front yard and even if we wanted to go in the opposite direction, we found ourselves making some detours and still ended up at the tennis courts.

Meanwhile Trust was losing the ball he had left the house with — for he never left the house without a ball, nor returned home empty-mouthed — so we always had to search until we found a ball. And you know, you can always find something if you think it's there and if you look hard enough and in the right place. Hence when you're looking for a ball by the tennis courts, chances are you'll find one. Especially if you have a Labrador nose, which can smell them from a distance, like truffles. He would stick his black nose under the vegetation and pull them out from places we wouldn't expect and where no one else could have found them.

Trust found a tennis ball almost every day, sometimes twice a day. He loved balls so much that he would take them in his mouth like something precious and well-deserved, and wagging his tail cheerfully, he would go home like a winner. His joy at the sight of a tennis ball was immense. And it happened every time and with every ball!

Trust's record for found balls was when we were in New York and he stayed home with Grandma. It had been the only time Trust was without us for more than two weeks. After the first week he started waiting for us at the gate, so Grandma took him out for repeated walks to take his mind off us.. When we returned, he sensed the taxi from the moment it entered our street and immediately went to the door. The joy of seeing us again cannot be expressed in words.

He took our scarves from around our necks and ran away with them, to prevent us from leaving again, as if we couldn't leave without them. We were eager to offer Trust and Grandma the souvenirs we had brought, and in return, they were eager to show us their new collection of tennis balls: a full basket. There were more than thirty balls! Good thing we got back in time, otherwise the tennis club would have remained without balls.

One by one, the balls were released from the confinement of the basket and set free.

In areas where tennis balls did not grow, the trophy was either a plastic bottle that had been thrown away (which then ended up being recycled), a large rock or a piece of wood. These trophies we didn't keep on display, we got rid of them as soon as he fell asleep, which happened fast after all that running and concentration.

When Trust discovered interesting scents, the tennis ball was forgotten and lost. Knowing that, we made sure we had a ball in the pocket, and when we wanted to return home and Trust had not found another ball yet, we discreetly placed it so that he could find it...The strategy shortened the search and the walk and also avoided bringing a new trophy into the house.

He was very happy to look for and find balls in places hidden from the eyes of hurried passers-by, but what he preferred was for someone to play fetch with him. Trust adored running after the ball, catching it and returning it to the thrower, because he was a Labrador retriever, and that's what retrievers do, they return everything they receive. And they perform it with the greatest dedication and with much, much joy. If someone wants to play with him, the Labrador is always ready and never refuses anyone.

Trust's joy at finding a ball was slightly greater than that of a major tennis trophy winner.

Perhaps in the long history of tennis tournaments, Labradors had played the role of ball kids, otherwise where did such skill and passion to collect and return tennis balls come from?

We imagined Trust's aristocratic ancestors, the English Labrador retrievers, running enthusiastically to find and return balls to the players on the pristine grass of Wimbledon at the inauguration of the prestigious tennis tournament in 1877.

**When you love what you do,
you live fulfilled.**

In the great fabric of life,
everything is interconnected and
interdependent.

A Christmas full of adventures

One Christmas Eve, we arrived in Constanța in the afternoon. We were expected at lunch by some dear friends, and then we were going to spend the evening with Cristi's mother.

We stopped directly at them, parked by the garden near their block of flats, and Trust gladly got out of the car and immediately began scouting the area to find out where we had arrived.

He exchanged a few glances with a Pekingese who was already there and then they both started wagging their tails, happy at the unexpected meeting. Our friends, coming out on the balcony to greet us, called Trust, and he answered by wagging his big, happy tail. We thought it would be good for him to hang out in the garden first, bearing in mind he had been in the car for three hours, so we left him with his new friend, a local as it seemed, and went up. From the window, we watched him curiously exploring the garden, and every now and then he looked up at the balcony where he knew we were and from where something delicious landed, because after all, it was Christmas Eve.

Both Trust and the Pekingese enjoyed the game. We were throwing food and they were looking for *the prey* and savouring it. It was like they were hunting. And in that way, both we and Trust enjoyed the delicious dishes, lovingly prepared for us. Just before we got dressed to leave we checked on Trust one more time. He was still there, waiting for us. But when we got down, Trust was nowhere to be found.

We thought he was on the other side of the garden and we started calling him out, but Trust didn't give any signs. We kept calling his name, our friends came down immediately and we looked for him together. We started searching around the block, then made larger circles. Nothing, no trace of him.

At one point, a neighbour who had heard our yells, came out to the window. She was living on the ground floor of the nearby block of flats and had seen everything. She told us that a few minutes ago she had seen a teenager pulling a dog tied with a rope. It was clear from her description that the dog was Trust.

'But where did they go?' we asked.

'Behind the dray!'

'Behind the dray!?' we exclaim bewildered. 'And where did the dray go?'

She didn't even finish saying that she didn't exactly know that we immediately spread out in all directions looking for the dray. We ran to where the street intersected with the boulevard. But no trace of Trust. It was getting dark, the public lighting was very poor and on top of that a fog was forming. Fearing that we might not find him right away, we decided we urgently needed to put up missing dog posters. We realised that if we hurried, we could still catch the nearby mall open, where we knew there was a photo centre and could print a picture of Trust.

Half an hour later, posters with his picture, our phone number and the reward we were offering were put up on all the doors of the blocks in the area.

We continued the search. We literally wandered the whole neighbourhood and the surrounding areas, without finding any trace of Trust. We were like tired carol singers who forgot the text of the carol and only repeated the chorus:

Trust, Trust, Trust,
Trust, Trust, Trust...

We felt like Kevin's parents in the well-known Christmas movie "Home Alone 2: Lost in New York."

It was already past midnight when, exhausted, we agreed that it was better to go and rest for a few hours, so that we could continue the search at dawn with fresh forces. With one last effort, we posted about Trust's disappearance on Violeta's facebook and on a few pet lover sites.

At dawn on Christmas day, I was suddenly woken up by Violeta, who was shouting and trying to open the window:

'Trust, Trust is outside!!'

I thought to myself that it would really be a miracle, considering that we had slept at my mother's place, who lived in another neighbourhood, a few miles away from where Trust had disappeared. We quickly opened the window and looked again, but when the dog got a little closer we saw that not only was it not Trust, but it was a Golden Retriever (those with longer coats than Labradors).

We have noticed how desires influence our perception and how we begin to see what we want to see.

The whole day continued at the pace in which it had begun: alert, searching, sometimes on foot, sometimes by car, and then on foot again, all the time shouting louder than carol singers.

Violeta's phone rang several times after posting Trust on Facebook. But the calls turned out to be false alarms: the dog had been found a long time ago, or it was a female, and sometimes when they sent a picture, it was not even a Labrador...

The more time passed, the harder it became for us. It was painful to accept that we would have to spend another night without any news about him. It was already evening, so we decided to let our friends know that we would not be able to spend the Christmas evening together as planned. No sooner had we done it than Violeta's phone rang again:

'We saw on Facebook that you lost a Labrador... we saw the picture and recognised him! He was running disoriented on the sidewalk last night and he followed us. We realised he was lost and took him in, to look after him.'

'Last night? What time was it? Where?...

We will come right away, please give us the address.'

The place described was several miles away from where Trust had disappeared, on the same boulevard, but at the other end. We jumped in the car and even though it was foggy and dark, we drove through town as fast as we could. The streets were empty, people resting after the hustle and bustle of preparing for Christmas.

When we arrived at the indicated place, although the fog had thickened, we saw them at once, on the other side of the road: two young men and a golden Labrador! We immediately turned the car around and stopped in front of them. We got out of the car impatiently to meet Trust. As soon as he saw us, he came towards us. We looked at one other. We couldn't believe it. It was Trust! We were all so enthusiastic. We opened the car's door and he jumped straight into his seat.

We asked the guys how we could reward them, but they assured us that there was no need. They confessed that they wished they had kept him, because they liked him a lot. But they were glad to return him because they realised it was the right thing for the Labrador to find his family, especially seeing how restless the dog was all night.

We thanked them wholeheartedly. We rewarded them and went away full of gratitude for having found Trust.

It's incredible how tiredness disappeared when we felt grateful.

Although we slept only a little and ran a lot, we felt refreshed. So we gladly went straight to our friends and rejoiced together that we had found Trust. It was wonderful to learn how many people had been praying to find him! We thanked those who helped us by sharing the Facebook post, and updated it from "lost" to "found."

Finding him was the most beautiful gift from Santa Claus. We couldn't wish for anything more.

In the morning, however, Trust was still restless and couldn't find his place. We then decided to return home to Bucharest, to his. environment, hoping that it would help him recover after everything he had been through.

Unfortunately, even when we got home, his condition did not improve. We kept wondering about what happened to him before he escaped from his captors and was found by the guys who called us. It looked like he had been forced to climb some stairs in a building, because since we got him back, he didn't want to climb stairs at all. But we didn't know what else he had suffered, he had no visible signs of violence, only that he was scared and had a cloudy, lost look.

We encouraged ourselves that a good night's sleep in his environment would do him good. We were right, he felt better but far from being the way he used to be.

We took him to his vet who had known him since he was a puppy. After consulting him, the vet said that it was obvious that Trust had been through trauma and that was why he was behaving strangely. The vet advised us to be patient and wait for his recovery. When he checked the microchip Trust had been wearing since his passport was made, he couldn't find it. He suspected it might be due to Trust spending so much time in the water..

I, Cristi, had accepted that it would take Trust a while to recover. But for me, Violeta, when the vet didn't find his microchip, it increased a fear that had been troubling me for some time: was it possible that he was not Trust after all and that was why he behaved so differently? Although physically it looked exactly like Trust, the dog's behaviour was different.

It would have been too much of a coincidence, however, that exactly a few hours after Trust had vanished, another Labrador appeared at the other end of the same boulevard, looking exactly like Trust and having the same age, according to the vet. Needless to say, he immediately jumped joyfully into our car.

However, I shared my fears with Cristi.

He couldn't believe what I was saying and asked me to be patient for a few days until Trust recovered. But for me, the thought that maybe it was not Trust was tormenting me.

So I asked Cristi in turn to consider that even though the Labrador looked exactly like Trust, it was highly likely that it was not our Trust, because he behaved in a completely different way.

It was the first time the two of us saw reality completely differently. It was awful. I realised that as long as Cristi was convinced that Trust needed a while to recover, he would not be able to accept the possibility that it might not be our Trust.

Realising what was happening, I tried to convince him that I was right. After several attempts to convince him, he firmly told me:

'This is the last time we talk about it, please accept that now Trust is like this and in the worst case maybe he would remain like this for the rest of his life, changed, different from how we knew him.'

Then I wrote in capital letters on a note: DON'T TELL ME I DIDN'T TELL YOU and I stuck it where it could be seen, on the refrigerator door.

Not knowing where Trust might be and with whom, and whether he might be hurt, hungry and desperately looking for us, was driving me crazy. The thought that maybe other people were desperately looking for their Labrador, while he was with us, also tormented me. So I posted again:

"We're still looking for Trust!"

Our friends asked me what was going on, because they didn't understand anything anymore: we lost him, we found him and now we're looking for him again? They also asked if he didn't have a collar by which he could be recognised. We told them that when we found him, the collar had been removed from his neck, and explained the strange coincidence of the physical resemblance, plus that he had been found the same evening wandering at the opposite end of the same boulevard near which Trust had disappeared.

They offered to post the announcement again in the hope that everything would clear up as soon as possible…

In a few days it was going to be the New Year and we were to leave for a mountain resort, where we had a hotel reservation.

I, Violeta, hoped that the friends we were going to meet there would also notice that the dog was not Trust. Their kids were very fond of Trust and I really thought they would realise it, but as soon as we arrived, they took him out to play in the snow like nothing was wrong. No one said anything, all of them thought it was Trust. Seeing that, I began to wonder if my mind was playing tricks on me, since everyone was convinced that it was Trust.

Late in the evening, I received a phone call. A man from Constanța who was walking his dog was stopped by some guys trying to sell him a Labrador! When he got home, he saw our post and immediately made the connection. He had recognised the resemblance with Trust and called us.

I asked him from the bottom of my heart if he could get their phone number. He assured us that he would go to the same area early in the morning to look for those guys and put us in touch.

It was very hard for me to know that the real Trust could be in Constanța, while we were in the mountains without him, right then on New Year's Eve. I was praying that the truth would come to light. And something did happen the next morning.

Our friends insisted that we should climb to the highest hill in the area to admire the view. We all walked through the snow, and when we reached the peaks, it was indeed a fairy-tale sight: all the valleys and hills were covered in a fluffy layer of snow, and the sun was shining very brightly for a winter day. The peace, clarity and joy of winter had spread everywhere, but it was still very difficult for me...

On the way back, as we were descending through the snow, I suddenly heard Cristi say in a very confident tone:

'Yes, indeed, he really isn't Trust!!'

Our friends and their children did not understand what Cristi was talking about. I hadn't told them anything, because I had hoped they would notice something different about Trust...

As soon as Cristi uttered those surprising words, his phone rang:

'Hello! Yes! How? When? Where?...Yes, yes! Wait there...about half an hour...I'm sending someone!'

We all looked at Cristi. His face was completely changed.

He told us that some gipsies claimed to have found our dog and demanded money to give him back.

The place they gave for the exchange was the same as the one described by the gentleman who had called last night! In addition, those guys had called Cristi's number which only appeared on the posters in the area where Trust had disappeared. Moreover, we had recognised their ethnicity by their voice, also mentioned by the neighbour who had witnessed the scene with the dray from the window. We knew then that they had taken Trust.

It had become clear to us: they had tried to sell him for a week and failed, and then they called us for the reward, right on New Year's Eve.

We immediately called someone from Constanța who knew Trust very well, explained to him what it was all about and asked him to go immediately to the meeting place.

Approaching the meeting place, he saw the guys holding Trust with a rope. A rope! Exactly as described by the lady who had seen them through the window when they took him.

He yelled from afar: Trust!!!

Then something extraordinary happened: Trust, with all his might, quickly pulled himself out of the kidnappers' grasp and ran at full speed straight towards his saviour, only stopping in his arms. Clearly at that moment, Trust realised he had found us too.

Seeing that they were together, Trust and our friend left joyfully, while the thieves shouted in unison: "the reward, the reward!" Afterwards they dared to call me again, reciting the same line: "the reward, the reward!"

I, Cristi, told them that when I would return to Constanța I would give them such *a reward*... They realised we figured out their scam and they did not have the courage to pursue the matter. They didn't even call for the reward. We were so content to know that we had found Trust and that he was fine! We hugged and cried with joy.

After crying, we burst out laughing when we realised we now had two Labradors:

> The real Trust at the sea,
> and his doppelganger,
> with us in the mountains!

Of course the fourth post followed:

> "Now we've actually found Trust
> and we have an extra Labrador!"

We attached a picture of him. We wanted to be able to find his family so that he could be at peace as well.

As by then we knew he was definitely not Trust, we began to see, in addition to the different behaviour we had noticed from the beginning, very small physical peculiarities, small distinguishing marks that differentiated the two *twins*. But as long as we thought he was

Trust, we hadn't noticed those very subtle differences.

It's amazing how our mind filters our perception of reality based on what we believe at that time!

✿   ✿   ✿   ✿

The next day early in the morning, Violeta's phone rang:

'Hello, I'm calling you about the Labrador! I just saw the picture you posted yesterday and I recognised him immediately, it's my Labrador, ours, the family's Labrador!'

We felt immense joy! We knew too well what it meant to find the Labrador after his disappearance from the family.

'We are very happy' — we answered — 'but what's his name?'

'Otto!'

'Otto??'

At that moment, the Labrador who was playing quietly on the carpet, suddenly pricked up his ears, raised his head and looked at us in a completely new way. He pricked his ears even higher, turning his head towards us. It was like saying: *you finally know my name! But how do you know it?*

We asked the gentleman to call him loudly and we put the phone on speaker. When the Labrador heard his voice, he stood up and began to search, puzzled and suddenly became so playful, you would think it was a different dog.

We request for a picture of their Labrador — which he promptly did. We were so thrilled by the likeness and hoped with all our hearts that it would be him. The gentleman gladly asked where we were, because he wanted to come and take Otto home. We told him that we were going to do it because after everything we had been through, we wanted to be absolutely sure, beyond any doubt, that he was really Otto, their Labrador.

We agreed when to meet and he gave us the address. They lived in Costinești, a seaside village and resort which was about 20 miles far from the place where we had taken the Labrador from the guys who had found him, on the night when Trust disappeared!

On entering their street, we stopped the car a few houses away from the indicated number. We had asked them to wait inside, to see if the Labrador would recognise the house and thus we'll be one hundred percent sure that the dog was Otto. We opened the car's door, the Labrador got out as usual, went to the first tree, started sniffing, went to the next tree still smelling, then suddenly stopped, as if frozen, and began to wag his tail very happily and with an amazing speed he ran away for about a hundred yards, with us following.

He stood up on his back legs and pushed hard against a gate... The gate recognised him and opened. It was clear that even the gate had been waiting for him. Otto triumphantly entered his own fortress, wagging his tail proudly, for he had found his lost nest.

It was fantastic to witness such a scene. What followed was as wonderful as his great entrance.

The whole family was out there, on the porch. They had tears of joy in their eyes. He immediately jumped towards them, full of joy. Many, many hugs followed.

It was as if their beloved son had returned from the battlefield where he had been reported missing without a trace. And yet, when everybody had given up hope, he returned as a brave winner. Even the family cat was happy to have Otto back. She really was!

We were welcomed into the house as saviours. That amazing reunion created such a beautiful atmosphere. The lady had just taken out of the oven her traditional *cozonac* – sweet bread with walnuts filling, specially made for that moment. Then, to celebrate that blessed winter day, we sat by the stove and listened to stories, while having a drink and savouring the sweet smell of the fresh, delicious *cozonac*.

They recounted how Otto had disappeared three months ago just from outside the house. The family had noticed some drays passing in the street and were worried that Otto was taken by those people. He used to go out into the street and to the beach by himself. They searched for days without stopping, extending their search to Mangalia, a city almost fifteen miles towards the south. It had been terrible. Day after day without any results. It was as if he had disappeared into the ground. Exhausted, after two months they had to stop searching and face the truth that they might never see him again, never be together again.

Then the miracle happened!

Friends of theirs who had seen the post shared by our friends, notified them immediately. We understood once again that life has its unknown ways most often incomprehensible to us humans at the moment when it happens. We understand some things later, others maybe never.

In this case, Trust's disappearance and everything that happened until he was found, led to the reunification of Otto's family when no one thought he would be found anymore. We were all so grateful. We knew that if Trust hadn't been stolen, Otto might have never made it home again.

Their daughter had received Otto as a precious gift for her eighteen birthday. We kept in touch with her all these years and from time to time, she would send us a picture of the lovely Labrador and would tell us how he was. For us, Otto will forever remain our *boy* too.

We have to trust that everything happens
for a reason, even if in that particular
moment we cannot understand it.

Some things seem incredible,
although they are absolutely real.

Trust and
the Magic of Life

An unforgettable day

Trust had a great quality, namely he was careful not to disturb and that made him loved and adored by so many people, and he also loved people more than anything.

The first and only time in his life when he met all the loved ones at once was at our wedding; almost everyone was staying in the same hotel as Trust. He loved being the centre of attention. One guest or another was constantly calling his name, stroking him and giving him treats and toys. Trust was so happy, he couldn't believe so many people that he loved were in the same place, all at the same time. He was running joyfully from one person to another, who were all eager to greet him and stroke his smooth, furry ears.

As some of the guests came accompanied by their furry friends, because they came to the seaside and couldn't leave their dogs back home, Trust was surrounded by some of his best friends. It was a real day of celebration. The people were relaxed, because the sea had a unique way of relaxing them. It was the middle of the summer, there was a holiday vibe in the air, so it was the perfect time to play with the amazing Labrador, who was also very young. It was really an unforgettable day for Trust and not only for him. For us it was great to know that Trust was busy with one of his favourite activities, socialising, being petted, massaged, in a word pampered. That gave us the time to get ready, because after all, it was an unforgettable day not only for Trust, but also for us.

We had arranged with a friend to bring Trust only at the end of the ceremony – which took place outdoors, at sunset, by the water – to take pictures with him. And as a Labrador who does not deny his nature, on his way to the place of the ceremony he found the only puddle in the whole area, in which he of course rolled.

When Trust appeared he looked cheerful, dressed festively and decorated with mud. He was such a presence. There was just us, the photographers and the purple sunset sky that was mirrored in the clear and quiet water. Trust was happy to be finally with us and stayed at our feet for the photo shoot.

He looked curiously at the camera, which made the job easier for the cameraman. Trust's face was radiating contentment. He was so beautiful in the sunset light with his bright and penetrating eyes. Around the neck he had a silk magenta scarf, like Cristi's tie – which matched perfectly his golden fur, and his relaxed and bohemian attitude seemed to say: *'I feel good in my skin, even though rolled and rigged out'*. Of course Trust felt that something was happening, he certainly sniffed our emotions. We stayed there for a while, the three of us, feeling content with what we were living. It was so wonderful to have him there with us, on an unforgettable day.

**The best reason for people to gather
is to celebrate Love.**

Talk from the heart
by Viggo Johansen

"You have found the Soul Mate,
and you can't hide it.
It radiates from deep within both of you,
shining through your eyes,
oozing from the pores of your skin –
and it's truly beautiful to See.

Even the dogs can feel it.

I watched you from the veranda yesterday.
You were taking a walk on the beach.
Cristi & Violeta and Trusty,
and then another dog a few meters behind.

It was such an atmosphere around you.

'They must be the happiest dogs in the world',
- I thought to myself -
living in the Love-bubble of Cristi & Violeta."

~ excerpt from the speech at our wedding ceremony ~

Trust the lucky one

As we have already said, Trust came with us everywhere except when we went on trips by plane. Then, because we couldn't take him with us, Violeta's mother came to stay with him. It was good for everyone: she loved coming to stay with Trust, we left home with peace of mind knowing she was safe and Trust, what can we say, was content with her. She spoiled him as only grandparents know how to do it.

So granny had an important mission, quite often. She was flying from Cluj specifically to stay with Trust. It was also a good opportunity to see each other, we spent a few days together before our departure and a few on our return. And thanks to Trust, we saw each other more often.

Granny was in a very good mood and on the way from the airport to our house she told us how well she felt on the plane, that she talked to the lady next to her the whole journey and they laughed a lot together. She played back their conversation:

'I'm going to Bucharest to see my grandson, because I haven't seen him for a year; I'm a little afraid of flying' , the lady told me.

'I'm also going to visit my grandson! I'll take care of him for a week. I come quite often because I like flying and I also like staying with him. He is handsome and kind and loves me very much.'

'How old is he?' asked the lady.

'Four and a half years', I answered.

'Do you have a picture of him?'

'Yeah sure! And I showed her the phone's screen on which I have Trust's photo.

'Oh, you fooled me', she said laughing.

'No, I didn't, not at all. I'm really going to be with him. I get along with him as if he were a child. He listens when I talk and when he tells me something in his own way, I understand him. We walk a lot and we both play with a ball. He also has a lot of common sense. If my phone rings while we're playing, he sits next to me and waits for me to finish my conversation. We can rarely find such good children nowadays.'

The lady listened so curiously, that she forgot about her fear of flying she had told me about at takeoff. I would have told her a lot more, but it was only a short flight.

Stories about Trust made even people
who had never met him feel joyful.

When we got home, the joy of seeing Trust again was immense on both sides, but manifested differently: Trust was running around, wagging his tail and bringing the toys from his basket one by one, as if to show granny that they had something to play with, and granny was taking goodies from Transylvania out of her bag, as if to assure him that they would enjoy a feast. They made a very good pair: Trust was responsible for the good mood and long walks in nature, and granny for the preparation of copious meals.

When everyone finished what they had to show, we all went by the lake, us walking and Trust exploring. Afterwards, we left Trust at home to rest by telling him we were going *hunting* — that meant we were going to bring him a treat — and I, Cristi, invited my ladies to dinner in the city. I had booked a table at the most famous restaurant of the day, in Charles de Gaulle square.

Violeta's mother and I chose one of their specialties, marinated meatballs in a delicious sauce. Very tasty, but the portions were so big that we couldn't finish them…even without the fried crust that I had put aside for Trust.

I asked the waitress to put what was left in a bag for our dog.

'Of course' she said, 'would you like to taste a dessert in the meantime?'

We enjoyed something sweet, then we paid the bill, got up, took the doggy bag and headed straight home with Trust in mind.

As we opened the door, Trust was jumping with joy to see us. Violeta didn't even get to open the doggy bag properly, when she saw a chilli pepper on top and said:

'Told them it's for the dog and they put chilli peppers?!'

Trust had already put his muzzle in the food when I looked into the bag and was surprised!

'A steaming portion of delicious *sărmăluțe* (traditional stuffed cabbage rolls) with polenta nicely garnished with a chilli pepper.'

By the time we figured out how those *sărmăluțe* had got to us, Trust was already wolfing them down, wagging his tail with joy. What a treat, what a delicious meal Trust received that evening! Lucky Trust!

We felt sorry for whoever got the leftovers, thinking that they were buying *sărmăluțe*. We could imagine him proudly calling his wife without suspecting what was really inside:

'I am home! I have brought your favourite food! Hurry up, it's still warm! Bon appetite!'

We had a lot of fun that evening doing all sorts of scenarios related to that confusion and

Trust was looking at us all the while licking his muzzle with satisfaction. He gained the most. Trust had been served a delicious portion of *sărmăluțe* with polenta decorated with chilli peppers, without attending a wedding (this food is customary at Romanian weddings).

We laughed as we imagined ourselves leaving the restaurant with a certain dish ordered for take away and getting leftovers, because confusions like this happen.

Such situations happen, and if we keep an open mind, instead of getting angry, we can have fun while life surprises us in various ways, because one thing is certain, it always does.

Life is unpredictable,
no matter how much we try to control it.

Trust's Magic word

We noticed that when we said the word ball, Trust would suddenly become very attentive. That word had a certain resonance in his mind that he immediately stood up, became alert, present and ready to play. It has always happened that way.

It would be wonderful if we too had such a magic word, and by simply hearing or saying it, to become **fully present and ready to live the fullness of life**. Thus boredom or illusory dreaming would disappear.

The closest words for us humans might be: **we are.** What can be more precious than the fact that **we are alive**?

❀   ❀   ❀   ❀

To Trust, ball meant any object that could be thrown by someone and held in his mouth. Those were the two conditions that qualified an object to be a ball.

It could be a plastic bottle, a toy of any shape, a stone, a stick, a seashell or even a snowball, in which case with each throw we made a new snowball to Trust's delight. And the game partner could be anyone who was willing to play with him, namely, catch the ball, throw it as hard as possible and wait enthusiastically until Trust brought it back from the water, from the snow, from the grass, from the sand...

Everything was very easy for him. It didn't matter if it was someone he knew or someone he had barely met, if the man was in the mood for a funny game and also had the time, he was the perfect partner.

Trust was tireless when it came to playing with the ball and was so dedicated to the game that he even forgot to eat. And for a Labrador, that was really a big thing, because they are known to be gourmet by nature. However, when it came to playing, Trust seemed to go beyond his gourmet trait.

We often felt that he fed on the joy of the people he played with, that he inhaled their happiness which he multiplied in his big heart and released it into the air, because Trust was a retriever, and a retriever always gave back what he got. After a game with Trust, everyone felt cheerful, energised and in good spirits.

The word ball was also magical for us. When we were busy and wanted to take him home but Trust would have preferred to stay outside, we used the magic word and he joyfully followed. And if sometimes that didn't work because he had played enough with the ball, we would go for the super magic word, namely: cat. He learned it from a young Greek, the owner of a hotel where we spent a holiday. He also had a Labrador which he was driving around the peninsula on his scooter.

We didn't know why he asked us how to say *cat* in Romanian, but we found out later that he wanted to tease Trust with that word. He kept repeating *the cat, the cat* until Trust memorised it as something important. When Trust heard it, he became interested and immediately came with us to help us find it. We were not sure what he expected to find, but the important thing was that he was coming in with us.

We never found a cat in the house, but we never gave up looking for it. So Trust had two words he couldn't resist hearing: the ball and the cat.

To his ears they sounded like something very important, something that could not be ignored, and to us they were magical because they always reached their goal. They were so powerful to him that when he was resting we were careful not to say these words, for he would immediately get up and come to bring us the ball or look for the cat.

**We are the ones who give meaning
to things and events.**

A surprise birthday cake

It was a sunny Sunday, early autumn, a day that couldn't be more beautiful because it was Trust's birthday. We were returning from the mountain resort, where we attended a course during the weekend in which, of course, Trust also participated, as in all our courses in the country. Besides being super qualified, he was also adored by all the participants, for his warm and quiet presence during the course and during breaks, ensuring good mood and relaxation. During our free time after classes, we could count on him to accompany us in exploring the area and getting to some less touristy spots. So he was a unique mountain guide.

And because sometimes life surprises us in a wonderful way, Trust's birthday coincided that year with the baptism of some dear friends' little boy.

Immediately after the class, all three of us in festive attire, Trust wearing a bow tie matching our outfit, we went straight to the party. When we arrived, the doorkeeper, seeing Trust in the car, asked us to leave the Labrador with him, so that he could have some fun. We were happy, as we were every time Trust brought smiles to people's faces. And that happened very often, meaning daily. It was good for Trust to sit outside in the shade, sufficiently distanced from the deafening music, but also close enough for those who wanted to see him.

When the waiter came to collect the plates, we asked him to put our leftovers in a doggy bag for our Labrador who was waiting for us in the yard, because we didn't like to throw away food. It was a pity to waste so many goodies; they really had the richest menus we ever saw. The waiter enthusiastically said that he would be pleased to serve the Labrador, because it was his job. He had already heard from his colleagues, about the cute Labrador in the yard, who plays football with the door-keeper. Lucky doorkeeper, we thought, to have the chance to play other roles, because Trust was the best *gatekeeper* in football. It was really cool to know that he was having fun too, after all we were at a party. And as you meet new people at parties, he also made a few friends. In truth, it wasn't hard at all for Trust to make friends because he was very friendly, and the first condition to have friends is to be a good friend first, which came naturally to Trust.

When we went to see how he was doing, we had a big surprise: Trust was contemplating a huge *cake* made of steaks, schnitzels, meat-balls, ham, salmon, bacon rolls and all kinds of cheeses. All those were carefully and skilfully placed in a mouth-watering *birthday cake*, decorated with great talent. The only thing missing was the birthday candle, but we realised that would have been useless as Trust wanted nothing more.

He was more than satisfied, he was touched. He was about a yard from the cake, looking at it with desire but also with restraint and caution, a little suspicious for fear it might be a trap. Little did he know that he would have a surprise birthday cake. It was too good to be true! He sat still, almost stunned, as if trying not to move much, lest he should wake up and find out it had all been just a dream. Occasionally, he found the courage to creep closer, take a piece with great care and precision, leaving the cake almost intact, retreat to a safe distance, not too far that he couldn't keep an eye on it, but not too close, just in case it was a trap.

There, he enjoyed every bite and kept an eye on the rest of the goodies, after which he got up and just as discreetly, took another piece. It was a real delight to see his bewilderment and at the same time delight at the unexpected feast. As usual, he took the pieces in order of his preference, because Trust always ate what he liked most first, never saved something he liked for later.

Trust's new friends, the waiters, were fascinated and amazed at how well-mannered their client was. They thought Trust would pounce on the goodies and devour them instantly. They told us that if they had customers like Trust every day, with common sense and manners, they would enjoy their job much more.

Trust had a cake every year for his birthday but that one remained memorable because it was a surprise birthday cake not only for him, but for us too.

**After every meal you have to give thanks
and be full of gratitude.
Always!**

Gratitude and joy of living
always travel together.

Travelling with Trust

The racing driver Trust

It was a very fine autumn afternoon, and we were driving leisurely through the sun-bathed hills of Dobrogea, a land where the vine feels at ease. The scenery looked enchanting in the sunset light. The vine, which not long ago had been laden with ripe grapes, now let itself be caressed by the gentle sun rays, and let its leaves be carried by the breeze. It had fully yielded her fruits, and then it allowed itself to relax, having fulfilled its purpose.

Trust, with his head out of the window, looked fascinated at the movement of the leaves, as if he too recognised the rhythm of the sea in that spectacular dance. We were returning to Bucharest after a summer at the seaside and without realising it, nostalgia had already settled into our souls...

Before crossing the bridge over the Danube river, as if trying to take with us something from the special bouquet of the place at that moment, we stopped to buy a good red wine, from a wine cellar of a famous vineyard. Due to the low visibility on that road, we left the car with the side lights on, the windows ajar and Trust sitting comfortably on the back seats.

We went to the entrance to see if it was still open, because no other car was parked there. We were lucky, even though they were preparing to close, they were glad to serve us, and they even gave us a little tour of the winery. They proudly presented us several types of red wine from the most appreciated grape varieties from which they then offered us samples to taste. We first admired the ruby colour of the wine, swirled the glass to aerate the wine and release its full aroma. Its rich bouquet delighted our senses. Seeing how much attention we paid to the tasting, they thought we were great connoisseurs and invited us into the cellar to see their precious collection of wines from the best years.

Their guess was not far from the truth, because we knew what qualities a good wine should have. We also knew something about growing vines from Violeta's father — who does this with lifelong passion — so we had the opportunity to learn a secret or two. We even planted vine cuttings, with Trust's help of course, who had learned to dig from his friend, the Archaeologist.

Fascinated by the impressive collection, we didn't even realise that it was getting really dark and foggy outside. We selected a good wine, full-bodied, fruity and fresh, from which to enjoy a glass with dinner quietly at home. Then we left the winery delighted with the hospitality shown to us and eager to return to Trust. Walking towards the place where we had parked, we noticed a woman staring at our car rubbing her eyes, as if she couldn't believe what she was seeing. We approached curiously, and when she saw us, she asked us, wonder struck:

'Is this your car??'

'Yes!' we answered. 'What's wrong?'

'I thought I was going blind!!' she said, still rubbing her eyes. 'Oh my goodness, it's so good that you came! Do you understand why I was staring?! I thought my mind was playing tricks on me! That I have visions, hallucinations... God forbid! I was hitchhiking, and I was so glad when I saw a car. I came quickly to ask the driver if he could give me a lift, but when I saw him I got really scared. Especially since there was no one else around...'

Behind the wheel was Trust!

The car lights were on, and Trust sat so naturally in the driver's seat, casually holding the wheel with his big paws and looking straight ahead, that it really looked like he was going to drive off at any moment! He looked like a racing driver waiting mindfully for the start. It was like a movie scene. We all burst out laughing. What a story!

If we had known earlier that we had a car with a chauffeur, we would have also enjoyed a glass of red wine in the famous winery.

Life simply happens.
Let's enjoy it!

Trust the Magician

In addition to being trustworthy, Trust had another great quality: It changed people's moods on the spot. And it's not just about ourselves. We weren't allowed to stay angry for more than five seconds anyway, because he would immediately come and push us with his big, black and wet muzzle, asking us with his gentle look: If you are upset, then what is my role here? In truth, it is almost impossible to stay angry around a Labrador.

Many times at traffic lights or in traffic jams when we saw sad or agitated people in cars, we would open the car's back window and Trust, curious where we were, would instantly get up and stick his head out the window. His large golden head attracted the eyes of the people in the cars like a magnet, who seemed to come out of their trance and look at him in amazement. Immediately there were smiles, some opened the window and asked us what breed he was and how old he was, others talked directly to him, some took pictures, and sometimes if the traffic light changed in the meantime and the cars started moving, they filmed him.

However, for a few moments everyone forgot about all the worries, the traffic jam, the fact that they were late. They lived in the moment briefly, without paying attention to the thoughts telling them they shouldn't be stuck there or they should be somewhere else. In fact, we were stuck in traffic, and no matter how stressed, agitated, nervous or bored we got, we were still there. Stuck in traffic.

The traffic jam was not impressed by our

restlessness, anxieties or desires. It was the way it was, whether we were agitated, irritated or glad to see a funny dog's head sticking out of a car window. And maybe sometimes, we became present for a moment, and realised we would get there when we were supposed to. Why should we insist on arriving sooner if life was showing us that such a thing was not possible?! Perhaps there were times when we hurried and even hurt ourselves or others, only to wish afterwards that we hadn't rushed.

However, life always went strictly according to its principles, it never deviated from them, for anyone. Therefore, wouldn't it be better to accept that? In the great fabric of life events happened exactly as they did, following the natural principle of cause and effect. As much as we wished that things were different, it didn't change anything. And if that was the case, then why struggle? Did it benefit anyone? Perhaps instead of stressing out, it could actually be a good time to review the day, to call a loved one or take a conscious breath...or maybe just admire a funny dog's head out the window of a car.

Occasionally, at traffic lights, he would suddenly change our mood, but in an unwanted way because he would suddenly bark very loudly when a beggar approached the car. Surely he didn't want to scare us, but the beggar, trying to convey to him that he had no business near the car. Only beggars and people dressed in certain uniforms or odd clothes were targeted by Trust. He had his reasons. And just once did he warn a burly train ticket inspector, (also called "godfather" in Romanian slang) who didn't like that Trust had bought a ticket… and that he wouldn't get any bribe.

**Events are forgotten,
but how people felt in your presence
will stay with them.**

The Heartfull Trust

One summer we were returning from the Danube Delta after staying at some friends' guest house, and we saw a puppy lying on the side of the road. He appeared to be dead, but when our car passed right by, he moved his head. We stopped to see if anything could be done for him. He looked like he had been hit by a car. He had no visible wound, but he was very frightened and weak and could not stand on his back legs. We realised that if he stayed on the side of the road in that heat, he wouldn't survive for long. Hoping that we might be able to save him, we took him to a vet clinic. Trust warmly welcomed him into the car next to him. It was the first time he was welcoming another dog on his back seat, until then he had only shared it with humans. We noticed once again the naturalness and curiosity with which Trust encountered new situations.

Unfortunately, the x-ray showed a spinal fracture that could not be operated successfully, according to the vet. We decided to foster him until we found a loving family to take care of him.

And because in his eyes you could read the desire to live, we named him Hope. He had much of a Cavalier King Charles Spaniel, small waist, longer silky coat, white with reddish brown spots. One of the spots was in the shape of a heart. He was an adorable puppy.

One day when we were returning home, a neighbour — who was not fond of animals — greeted us amazed and told us that if she had not seen it with her own eyes, she would never have believed it. She told us that she saw Trust and Hope sitting on the terrace of our apart-ment and at one point Hope tried to crawl towards the water bowl but couldn't make it. Trust seeing him struggling, went to the bowl and started pushing it with his muzzle towards Hope. He did that so carefully that he managed to carry it without spilling the water. That was extraordinary! We realised that animals could teach us a lot about humanity.

It wasn't the first time Trust surprised us with something hard to believe, even impossible for those who weren't lucky enough to live around a furry friend.

Once, when a dear friend who had come to Bucharest for an eye surgery was staying with us, she excitedly told us what Trust had done while we were away.

As she sat on the couch, both eyes bandaged, she felt Trust's whiskers and breath on her hand. Then, she felt his wet, cool muzzle discreetly touch her and drop something into her hand. It was a tennis ball. She was so happy because Trust had been playing with her companion before, putting the ball at her foot. They started playing throw and catch, and it was obvious that Trust adapted the game to the situation. She was fascinated by how Trust had found a new kind of game that she could participate in too. She was trying to understand how Trust knew she couldn't see? And how did he know to put the ball in her hand every time after she threw it? And how did Trust always knew to leave it at his companion's foot, never in her hand?

We have to admit, we were also impressed by Trust's way of adapting and interacting differently depending on the game partner. He showed us once again that he was a good host who offered each guest a game that suited them.

Trust had also shown us how welcoming he was when our neighbours' two-year-old boy came to play with him. We served him white seedless grapes, but he was interested in putting the fruits in Trust's mouth. We told him they were for him because Trust didn't eat grapes, but the kid kept feeding him. Trust, seeing how much the child wanted him to eat them, began to take one grape at a time from the child's hand, much to his delight. Seeing how that brought joy, he ate the whole bunch. Each grape taken by Trust, made the child laugh out loud. It was like we had a jukebox that worked with grapes instead of coins and the tune was the little boy's chuckles. We were also caught up in his merriment, so it was a very cool visit.

The next day at breakfast we showed Trust the grapes to see his reaction. He looked at us indignantly, as if saying: 'Come on... Did you not realise that I only ate to entertain the child?' Indeed, it was the first and only time Trust ate grapes. Afterwards, when we recounted the story to our vet friends, they told us that it was recently discovered that grapes can be toxic to dogs.

With every event in which Trust showed his human qualities, we understood better that he felt the human vibe with accuracy; since the vibe doesn't lie. That was why he was able to be so empathetic. He could smell the state people were in and respond accordingly.

We would often look at him and say to ourselves: Nature created a masterpiece through Trust! It must have practised a great deal until it managed such perfection! We wouldn't have changed anything about him, not even a hair.

Hope was adopted by Violeta's brother and his wife, a very loving family. With the help of a small stroller that supported his back legs, Hope succeeded in becoming the fastest dog. The joy and determination with which he ran was touching and uplifting. Besides being very likeable, the way he moved conveyed will and courage. His joy of life was also a true inspiration for those who passed by his gate and saw him.

He lived on for nine years, loved by all the family, including Trust's Granny, who became his Granny too, and by everyone who knew his story.

Life always finds new ways to live!

Trust in Transylvania

We often travelled to Transylvania and naturally, Trust came with us. Our friends and family loved him so much that we were not sure that we would have been welcomed without him.

One beautiful late August day, we set out on one of those trips. Wanting to avoid the busy roads entering the cities and to see new places, we decided to search for a different route.

All said and done, we looked for and found an alternative route on Apple map, which looked interesting. It was taking us near woodlands where we were able to walk Trust freely. Besides, it promised to shorten the distance to the destination. But it was certain that we would not have a very smooth asphalt road.

Satisfied with the result of our search, we followed the app's instructions. At one point, we entered a village where time seemed to stand still. Everything had a fairytale appearance, untouched by technology. The asphalt ended abruptly and was replaced by a cobbled road. Just as suddenly, the internet signal stopped, without having had the opportunity to look at the map in more detail.

Fascinated by those picturesque lands, far from the hustle and bustle of the big cities and the rush of the main roads, we pull over the car with the intention of walking Trust and to admire the scenery more.

Up the road, a small group of boys were playing football. A few cows were lazily crossing the street. Birds of all kinds were singing a symphony known only to them, but easily perceived by whoever was willing to pause and listen. The air bore a ripe, rich aroma, both familiar and new, as if more intense, emanating from the juicy grapes sunbathing on the roofs. Everything embodied the message:

Life is beautiful,
take time to delight in it.

🐾 🐾 🐾 🐾

Our contemplation was soon interrupted by a thud. A cyclist, slowly pedalling a bicycle that appeared to belong to another century, passed by our parked car, gazed at Trust's head sticking out of the window, overtook us on the right, rode a few more yards then lost his balance and fell straight down in the ditch on the side of the road.

We quickly jumped out of the car to help him get up, but he immediately got up like a roly-poly toy. We asked him:

'Are you OK…? What happened…? Why did you fall?'

'Oh, well, what can I tell you… I didn't

expect you to be here!!.... I looked at the car, I looked at the dog and before I knew it I was in the ditch... I am ok, I am sturdy. It's not the first time nor the last when I take a fall. Don't worry about me!'

After we said goodbye, he resumed riding, leaving us astonished and amused by his answer: 'I didn't expect you to be here!'

Meanwhile, the boys playing football nearby saw Trust and approached with curiosity. While they were petting him and playing with him, we asked the eldest of them:

'Do you know how long it is to get to the first town?'

'Oh, it's not much longer!'

'Is it near?'

'It's not that close!'

'But do you know how many miles there are?'

'There are quite a few!'

'So it's close!?'

'It's not far...!'

'But is the road good?'

'It's good!'

'Is it paved again!?'

'Oh no, it's not!'

We could hardly stop laughing, especially when we saw that even Trust, who had listened to the dialogue with all his attention, looking from us to the boys and back, was just as confused as we were. It was a very funny and not at all helpful discussion. We went on laughing, determined to give the route one more chance up to the top of the hill in front of us, where the village ended.

But, surprise: not only was the road not asphalted, but it wasn't even paved! We found ourselves on a dirt road with no settlement in sight and no signposts to the next village. And as if that was not strange enough, near the top of the hill, coming from the other side, four people were pushing a dusty car up the road.

Trust, who was travelling with his head out of the window, although very attentive to what was happening, still did not identify what was approaching us. It looked like a car, moved like a car but it didn't sound like one... It was moving slowly towards us, and when it reached the top of the hill, it came to a halt. With the sun directly behind it, it was easy for Trust to mistake it for an animal. So he stood very alert lest the strange animal should make any sudden movement.

With its dusty hood resembling a shell, and the four men pushing from the sides as its legs, the vehicle looked like a giant turtle. Anything was possible in that new place in the middle of the wilderness, especially seen through Trust's innocent eyes…

He had heard from a Chihuahua who had travelled by plane to many exotic places — being so small it easily fit into a pocket — that giant turtles lived in the Seychelles.

Back then he had thought that the Chihuahua was exaggerating, that the turtles looked so big because he was so small, but at that moment he began to believe him: *perhaps the turtles that lived in small waters remained little, like those with which I swam daily in my yard pond, and they became gigantic only when living in big waters like the ocean. So the Chihuahua didn't lie* — Trust admitted and he promised himself that one day he would give the Chihuahua more credit, even though he was so tiny that he fitted into a pocket.

Trust felt lucky to have two turtles among his friends, because he had heard that they lived for hundreds of years, and that meant friends for life.

As they approached Trust realised they were humans — and therefore friends of his — so he started wagging his tail gladly.

Seeing Trust, with his golden and merry head sticking out of the window, those who were pushing the car suddenly stopped, and the car was about to slide down the valley, just like in a Louis de Funès comedy.

'Shall we tow you?' we offered.

'Aaah, thank you...no, there's no need now. Now it's easy, we take the car downhill and then it starts!'

Hearing his confident answer, we deduced it had happened before.

'Is the way forward good?' we asked.

'It's good!' he said.

'But aren't there big pits?'

'Yes, there are.'

'How many miles is it to the paved road?'

'Well, there aren't many of them, we're going all the time.'

Again, the answers were as clear as mud. However, inspired by their determination by repeatedly pushing upwards a car that didn't function all the time, we decided to venture further, since it was our turn to take the easy way downhill.

Indeed the people were right: the road was neither long nor short, neither bad nor good, and the next town was neither far nor close by.

Although we also ended up with a super dusty car, it was well worth the trip back in time. The fact that we chose to try a new path opened the possibility to experience something new. It was an unforgettable adventure, without internet signal, but connected directly to the incomparable Transylvanian humour.

Those trips with Trust in Transylvania were great. Life surprised us in various ways and we experienced events that would become unforgettable memories.

When seen with fresh eyes, the moment
opens up and life appears differently.

True home is not in a physical place,
it is right in the calm of our heart.

Trust's Adventures in Greece

A hilarious confusion

Planning to visit a large part of the main-land Greece with an electric car can be an adventure in itself, but when you also have a Labrador retriever as a passenger, it's clear that you're in for a lot of adventures.

It was an informed decision, we knew that Greece did not yet have an infrastructure for fast charging of electric cars, but we knew that we were not in a hurry to get anywhere and we also wanted to see more places in that region. We intended to cover shorter daily distances than how we travelled other times, to enjoy the wonderful places there and to charge our car at the hotels we would spend the night at.

The final destination of the trip was Pelion, where we were going to meet our friends and spend some time together. And of course to celebrate Trust's birthday the way a Labrador should be celebrated, which is by the seaside.

In September, the azure sea was warm and inviting, and the landscapes were spectacular. Our road wound along the coast, with the mountain on one side and the sea on the other. Everything was absolutely perfect, we couldn't have asked for anything more and Trust was content and amazed that he could swim at every stop.

The advantage of travelling at that time of the year is that you don't need to book in advance. The peak season had passed and that gave us the freedom to stay a night or more in one place, depending on how it suited us, without having to arrive somewhere the next day.

The only reservation we had was in Pelion.

We started our trip a few days earlier than the rest of the group we were going to meet, so we had time to discover charming places to come back to and enjoy some time there. Of course, we only chose hotels that welcome pets, as was the case of the hotel where we were going for our next stay. It was the second accommodation since we started our adventure in Greece.

At the first hotel where we spent the night, Trust was warmly welcomed, the car got electricity, and we were spoiled with delicious Greek food. Above all the room offered a magnificent view of Mount Olympus. It was a unique experience to have the sea in front and the legendary Mount Olympus a few miles behind. We planned to come back another time to explore the area properly as it really was impressive.

Leaving there on the cool of the morning, we arrived shortly before noon at the next hotel on our itinerary. It was an unexpectedly hot day for that time of year, so the first thing we did was find a green area to walk Trust, then we sat down on the cool, shady patio of the hotel, waiting for the check-in time.

We used the time to search online for the next hotel we would spend the night at, which would fit the distance of our car's range. Meaning, it should not be too close — for we still had a long way to Pelion — but not too far so we could still get there directly without another charge. Sometimes we found the next place right away, sometimes it took longer. But we knew from Trust that in life if you want to find something, you have to look for it long enough and in the right places. So we never lost hope.

When it was time to check in, we went to the reception to get the key. Trust curiously went in to explore the new place, but as he met the pleasant coolness of the air-conditioned air, he relaxed and left the exploration for later. He had also played earlier outside with a lot of people, so a siesta was more than welcome.

The receptionist saw him and told us with a scared face:

'He is not allowed in the hotel!'

'How is that possible?!' we asked in disbe-lief. 'On your website it's written that this is a pet friendly hotel, that's why we chose it.'

We look at her in bewilderment.

She insisted:

'A pet!' and she showed us her water bottle.

We didn't understand what she meant by that...But suddenly we realised that by the word pet she was referring to something the size of a PET (plastic bottle).

At first we thought she was joking, but we soon realised she was very serious. Trust had to be as small as a PET to fit into a large hotel. And as it was impossible to shrink Trust and not wanting to spoil our good mood, we went out on the terrace of the restaurant to have lunch and in the meantime to search online for a truly pet friendly hotel.

While we were waiting for our food, we wondered if the rooms at this hotel were really as nice as we had seen them on the website when we made the reservation, and made us go a little out of our way to stay a night there.

So I, Cristi, was curious to see a room. I went to the reception and they gave me the access card for the room.

I opened the door and I saw a luxurious room with the curtains half drawn, on the table between the armchairs a bottle of champagne next to a basket of fruit, and the double bed was only partially visible, as was **the naked man who was lying face down in it!!!**

I couldn't believe what I was seeing in front of my eyes! From the position he was in, there was no way he could see me, and because he didn't get up in surprise, I could tell he hadn't even heard the room door open. Thinking I'd entered the wrong room, I tiptoed out, slowly pulling the door behind me. I took a deep breath of relief when I checked the number on the card and the number on the door: it was the same!

I went straight to the reception, where in the meantime the woman who was running the hotel had arrived. I handed them the card and told them directly:

'There's a naked man in the room!'

They froze. Then they stared at each other, hoping that maybe they misunderstood what I was saying, considering that I was speaking in

English. I assured them that they understood well:

'There is a naked man in the room !!!' I exclaimed in a very convincing tone.

Ashamed and confused, they didn't know what to say. Agitated, red-faced, they spoke quickly to each other in Greek, gesturing amply. I was amused, but trying not to show, as I was expecting an explanation. Maybe those were the house rules, Greece being usually invaded by foreign tourists, you never knew...

They offered thousands of apologies ... and to make up for it, they handed me the access card to their most luxurious apartment and kindly asked me to forget the unwanted incident. The receptionist, trying to avoid another blunder, drew the manager's attention to the fact that we had a dog with us that was bigger than a PET!

'What dog? The Labrador on the terrace?... Trust?' she asked, suddenly becoming cheerful.

'Yes, him!' I replied surprised that she knew his name.

'I just met him and played with him. He's adorable!'

So, in an unexpected way, everything suddenly changed. From not being welcomed with Trust in the hotel —because he was bigger than a PET — to being accommodated in the most luxurious apartment with a more than generous terrace for Trust to feel at ease.

It was interesting to note that if we had immediately left there dissatisfied with the receptionist's refusal, it would have been impossible to enjoy what life unexpectedly brought.

Before long, Trust, who had misplaced his ball and taken a PET from the terrace instead, was triumphantly walking past the front desk wagging his tail and holding the PET proudly in his mouth.

It was clear! Trust understood something from all that nonsense and as he knew that the receptionist did not want a dog in the hotel, but only a PET, he brought her one.

The moment just happens!
Our reaction to it closes or opens
the possibilities we can experience.

We explore ancient lands with Trust

Every time we were arriving with Trust in a new place, we fondly thought of the words of a friend: "Do you realise that Trust has seen more countries than I have?!". And so it was when we arrived at the giant plane tree of Pelion, possibly the oldest and largest tree in Europe. Even Trust looked like a Chihuahua under the huge plane tree.

You could tell that the venerable plane tree lived in peace and enjoyed its life to the fullest, it had grown harmoniously in its natural rhythm, without hurrying to reach higher. In its so generous shade, hikers stopped to catch their breath in a moment of contemplation.

Legend has it that in the past people tested the place by planting a plane tree and if it took roots it was considered a favourable place for a settlement. Looking at this amazing plane tree, we understood why the great Spanish architect Antoni Gaudí had plane trees as a source of inspiration when he designed the Sagrada Familia, the symbol of Barcelona.

But now we were curious what Trust would do, how he would approach *marking* the giant plane tree. We thought he was in trouble, he didn't know exactly whether it was in the tree category or the building category, because in addition to being as big as a villa, it also had a stone pillar supporting an arm. So Trust stood amazed and watched it, not believing what he was seeing. It was as if he was saying to himself: *Now my friend Chihuahua will not believe me when I tell him that I saw a really huge tree. But if he doesn't believe me, he can just look at my Instagram page!*

A few days before, we and Trust had been fascinated when we arrived at a cotton plantation for the first time. We didn't even know that cotton was also grew in Greece. The joyful cotton flowers, of an immaculate white, stood gracefully facing the sun. Trust was very curious what kind of *balls* were these: so many, so fluffy and so soft. He had never seen anything like that.

After that fascinating stop, we left Pelion for the Pindus mountains, intending to stop for a night in Metsovo. A friend who had often come to the region, recommended a good accommodation with a friend of hers. It sounded good, it was an eco-boutique hotel, so we went there. In Metsovo, as in many other ancient mountain settlements, apart from the main road, the rest of the roads are very narrow. Our car crept up until we arrived in front of the chic hotel and when we wanted to park we saw an entrance going down to the basement. Trust was looking in wonder out of the window, telling us with his eyes: *where are we entering? Do we fit in here? From my window the wall feels very close, I touch it with my whiskers, I better pull my head in quickly!*

After a very short time, the owner of the hotel, who was waiting for us to arrive, came down. We sensed his surprise when he saw us and we thought our friend hadn't told him we had a Labrador with us. But no, it wasn't about that, because he immediately began petting him and asked us what his name was. Now, that the introductions had been made, we also found out why he was surprised:

'Is the car purely electric?? It's the first time I've seen one in reality!'

When he found out that it was pure electric, he urged us to park the car and invited all of us in, so he could ask for more details. We were curious how we were going to get the car out of there, of course in the event that we would manage to enter the parking lot through the stone walls which were so close and get through the sloped curve.

So the adventure of going underground began. Suddenly the hotel owner signalled us to stop. By the time we realised what was happening, the car simply started spinning while we watched as surprised spectators.

Even more surprised was Trust, whose face we could see in the mirror: He stared intrigued and amazed at our spinning car and did not understand what was happening. Never before in his entire dog life had he seen something like that!

At the entrance to the ingenious underground parking lot there was a rotating ramp that turned our car around to our designated parking spot. At one point, our host pressed the stop button and signalled us to park the car, in the only place we had access to from that position. We were pleasantly impressed by the creativity with which they had transformed a hard-to-reach basement space into a much needed parking lot.

He was looking at our electric car like at a UFO and was keen to find out more. When we asked him for access to an outlet, he was downright amazed. He didn't think that the car could be charged from a normal outlet. He was convinced that his dream of having an electric car in Greece could be fulfilled only after enough years, when special charging stations had been installed.

He really wanted a quiet and non-polluting car because he liked green things, as we could tell from the name of the hotel. And in addition, was remarkable to be able to charge his car in his own garage without having to cross to the other side of the mountain for the gas stations.

The discussion continued in the morning, at the hearty breakfast with local organic products. Our host was curious to go down to the car to see if it was really charged. When he saw that the charging worked perfectly, he told us:

'You know... I've been thinking all night... don't laugh at what I'm going to ask you... how about selling me the car?? I really like it and it would fit perfectly here...'

He didn't have time to continue because we were both laughing. The image of the shepherd from Meteora who a few days ago wanted to buy Trust came to our mind. And now were we getting an offer for the car as well?

It was a good thing we didn't give Trust away, because we could ride him back home with luggage and everything!

We knew of the commercial skills of the inhabitants of those lands, but we did not expect that they would want to buy both our dog and our car, and that at such a short stay. He laughed heartily when we told him that we had also had a buying offer for Trust.

As soon as we got out of that surprising parking, Trust quickly jumped into the car, eager to continue our trip. He seemed very glad that we didn't sell the car and that we didn't have to ride on him all the way home with our luggage on his back. Trust was big and stubborn at times, but still he was not a mule!

**The so-called little events are not small at all.
They give colour and flavour to our life.**

Trust and Meteora

We had chosen to end our holiday in Greece with two quieter days in Meteora. We booked a good hotel with a direct view to Meteora, pet friendly and which, to our surprise and joy, also had a charging station for electric cars. It was the first time that a hotel in Greece had that, and they proudly wrote it on the hotel website. Enthusiastic that we were to go to Meteora, we set off, and Trust, sensing our joy, was very curious as to where we would end up next.

We crossed the wide plain of Thessaly until the mountains came into view again. And just as we were approaching Kalambaka, suddenly we saw in front of us the impressive Meteora, in the special light of the sunset. It was absolutely fascinating.

We stopped the car to contemplate that never-before-seen landscape. The rays of the sunset bathed the whole place and illuminated the monasteries that had been up there on the ridges for hundreds and hundreds of years. We understood then why the place is part of the UNESCO World Heritage Site.

All those wonders of nature, standing still and immovable, watching as if from eternity as a silent witness of the flow of time that carrying with it the change — of human civilisations, beliefs, convictions and customs. They also seemed to watch over the villages lying at their feet.

We delightfully went on our way, looking forward to arriving, so we could leisurely contemplate those wonders, in the colours of the twilight, and unravel their secrets.

Following the route to the hotel on Google maps, we entered at one point on an unpaved road, which climbed a high hill, through a forest of lianas. The road was very rough and bumpy, as if a great flood had shattered it. We wondered how a hotel as good as we had seen it on the website had such access. We thought we might have gone the wrong way, but the map showed us we were on the right track even though it seemed like we were on another planet considering the scenery around us. The so-called road passed through small Meteors that Trust looked at curiously, wondering what they might be?

We finally reached the top of the hill, where instead of a hotel there was only a deserted plateau, except for a sheepfold in front of which stood a shepherd with his sheep, sheep that looked more like goats, although they were not goats.

Strange, however, no sign of the hotel,

although the map showed it was there. We wanted to go back and start our search anew but we immediately realised that there was no internet signal. We were almost convinced that we had taken the wrong road, although the map showed otherwise. Besides all that, the car's electric battery indicated that we were on reserve. So it was clear that we could no longer continue the adventure into the unknown.

The shepherd leaned on his stuff and looked at us smiling. His smile conveyed more satis-faction than surprise. He must have been amused that we had wandered there, we thought. We almost got it: he was amused by how many tourists were wandering around looking for that hotel. After we greeted each other and started talking, he told us half jokingly, half seriously:

'I would have gained much more to turn the sheepfold into an agro-tourist guesthouse, given how many tourists have arrived here over the summer looking for this hotel...'

But he was too used to his sheep and couldn't be bothered. While we were talking, Trust had already made friends with the sheep and was studying them closely very curiously: *strange sheep* — Trust seemed to say too — *did not resemble at all with my sheep friends from Transylvania. It's like they have goat faces.*

And we were still curious about them… what kind of milk would they give if they looked exactly like sheep but had the face of a goat? It was clear, they were the secret of the famous feta cheese. Although the Greeks told the whole world that the delicious feta cheese was obtained from sheep's milk and goat's milk, no one has ever managed to make a feta cheese as good as theirs. Obviously, these goat-faced sheep had to be the secret. They certainly gave feta milk directly!

All the while the shepherd also looked curiously at Trust, he couldn't believe how well he got along not only with the sheep but also with his dogs. He asked us if we had a cigarette, we told him we didn't smoke. He asked us what breed the dog was, and said that Trust was the first foreign dog that his sheep were not at all scared of.

'English Labrador retriever', we proudly told him.

He had heard of the breed, but had never seen a Labrador. Suddenly he told us:

'I have a large flock of sheep, wouldn't you like to sell me your Labrador because I could really use some help?'

Barely refraining from laughing, we questioned him about the number of sheep he was prepared to give us in exchange for Trust, and if he had more than the ones we could see there.

When he realised we were joking, he chuckled:

'Well, if I give you all my sheep, what do I need a dog for?'

We all had a good time, and Trust had been very close to finding his value in sheep.

The meeting with the shepherd was so fine that in those minutes we didn't care at all whether our car battery would be enough to return to civilisation. The mobile phone was also completely useless because it no longer had a signal, and the internet was out of the question. The good news was that to get back to the main road we had only to go downwards, so the car battery was going to charge. What happened was exactly that, and the car's computer recalculated the range. When we got back to the European road, we took a deep breath of relief.

Going the other way now, we saw a discreet wooden signpost which signalled the hotel. We followed the sign and arrived shortly. It was indeed a beautiful new hotel and it even had a splendid view of Meteora. There was no other building around it, and the whole hill was full of vines and olive trees, and in the courtyard there were fig trees and hydrangeas. It was enchanting.

We put the car on charge in the specially designed place and entered the hotel. We told them what happened, that we followed the map and arrived in the middle of nowhere. They apologised a thousand times. They knew about the wrong location on the map, from other customers who had experienced the same thing, and told us "they wrote to Google but have not received any response." We offered to help them correct the position on the map and they were very grateful. Had they known it was that simple, they would have corrected it since the opening of the hotel.

It was unpleasant to hear from customers that they arrived by car in the middle of nowhere. And if you also had an electric car with an almost empty battery and no signal on the phone, it proved quite challenging. But the hotel manager assured us that we were the first with such a car that arrived at the newly inaugurated hotel.

We were glad to check in so that we would finally be able to take a shower after all the adventures in the scorching heat. We turned on the water, which unluckily became gradually cold. We waited, but the hot water still didn't come. We called the reception, having expectations from a new 4-star hotel. The receptionist told us:

'I'm so sorry sir, but we have a problem. Something happened and the hot water plant lost power. But it's being solved now that we've figured out where the problem started: at the electric car charging station.'

We had a good laugh at the comical situation, so that was how things worked, we had to get down to unplug the car...so that the shower would work?!

All that time, Trust that had none of those problems sat quietly on the terrace and contemplated Meteora. To our joy, we soon joined him. The hot water came back on, they gave us another outlet for the car, so everything returned to normal.

The three of us sat gratefully on the terrace of our room, contemplating the warm twilight that was covering that fairytale land. Meteora seemed to whisper without words **what it was like to endure beyond time, to remain steadfast, as a witness silently watching all the changes of the times, knowing what truly counted in the rush of civilisations.**

We stayed outside until late that evening. **The sense of steadfastness and fulfilment that we experienced was actually emerging from our own being.** Meteora had only served as a mirror for something that was already within us.

When our thoughts no longer ran to the past or the future, to that or to the other, we were fully present there.

In that presence and with that clarity we were able to reflect together on what is really important in life.

That evening, we found out more about the essence of being human and acknowledged how precious and unique the gift of life is.

We realised that in our everyday life, there were so many moments when looking into the pure, deep and innocent eyes of Trust, they had the same mirroring effect for us, as Meteora.

They magically were deepening access to our being and were connecting us more profoundly with the warmth and clarity that are always present within us, where nothing exists separately, nothing has an existence of its own.

The only place where we find what we really seek, what matters, what does not change throughout our lives, what endures in the midst of change.

Here we find also that precious inner knowing, the wisdom that we need so much to guide us in the sacred journey of Life.

It is good to remind ourselves as often as possible,
how precious is the life we have.

The time will come

The wonderful Labrador retriever Trust was turning ten and he was to be nowhere else but at the sea, because when you say Labrador you also say the greatest water lover and an excellent swimmer. They have webbed toes like ducks for a good reason and their big, thick tail acts as a rudder while swimming. Their ancestors helped the fishermen by pulling the fish nets ashore. They were very helpful being strong, good swimmers and also very diligent. They are always eager to be of service to their human companions and to feel included in the team.

That time we had chosen a quiet bay in the Balchik area, to have a shorter drive, and to make it easier for Trust who had an honourable age in dog years. He was already walking more slowly, and his daily walks had many stops. It was as if he carried with him all the memories he had lived. And there were many, because he had a life lived to the fullest.

Although we were staying in an apartment right on the seashore, the walk to the beach was a real hike for him.

But when he entered the sea, everything changed: the sea, Trust's forever friend, took all his weight, and he was light, swift and full of life again.

You could read in the gleam in his eyes that he felt young again, lively and free from the burden of years. He felt supported by the sea as if by someone he trusted, he swam with the ease with which he once ran. Sometimes he would simply let himself go, and the water would take him a little into the sea, then bring him close to the shore, and so on. There was a beautiful dance between them.

The sea must have been very fond of Trust,

for it remained warm, calm and peaceful the whole time we were there. There was so much joy on Trust's face when he was in the water, that we extended our stay there.

One day a local fisherman came to us and asked if he could pet Trust. We were used to hearing such a question, because we heard it often. The fisherman looked at him very fondly and stroked him gently. At one point we noticed that he had tears in his eyes. He told us that his Labrador, who was his companion for ten years, had recently passed away. He asked us how old Trust was and with a lump in the throat we told him that he had just turned ten.

The next day, on our way to the sea, we met an older couple walking a Poodle. Seeing Trust they approached us. While the Poodle was socialising with Trust, they told us that they had also had a Labrador who shortly after turning ten fell ill and suddenly died. They advised us that when time will come for Trust to pass away, we shouldn't make the mistake of waiting long until we got another dog. They did that and they were left with their biggest regret…

Only after five years did they get the Poodle, realising that they had deprived themselves of the joy of living with such a friend for so long. "We wasted five years of our lives, don't do the same..." they told us.

We felt the sincerity with which they told us their story and we realised how much truth that understanding of theirs carries in it. We promised ourselves that when the time came, we would keep it in mind. In the place of a dog that leaves, much love remains and love cannot be stopped, love must go on…

It's so good when we manage
to learn from the experience of our peers,
without making the same mistakes.

Instead of the end

There is a myth that cats have seven lives. We don't know for sure about cats, but we do know that some Labradors can have three lives. At least that was the case with Trust. Or at least that was how we felt each of his returns, like a new life, like a new chance to live beautifully together, to enjoy his capers, to gather some unforgettable memories and understandings about the always surprising Life.

We felt that for the first time during the period described in the chapter "A Christmas full of Adventures".

We didn't know if we would ever see him again. But life was generous and we found each other, it was like a new life. And even though it was terribly painful for us, after the fear passed, we could see how it all led to something wonderful, Otto's return home.

We thus saw again, how **in life nothing is separate, everything is part of the same whole.**

The next time, it was when he got babesiosis from a tick bite, and at the veterinary clinic in Constanța — where we were when he suddenly felt sick — we were told: "you came too late." We were told that in a tone that suggested that Trust was already dead. Fortunately, that was not so. We drove to Bucharest and went to his vet. He and his wife, with great dedication and skill, did every-thing they could to save him even if the chances were very small. And because Trust was then a young dog who loved life very much, they succeeded. We are very grateful to them.

He was with us through thick and thin, at work and on walks, always at dinner time, at all kinds of events and on all holidays (except the ones by plane).

And we learned a lot about ourselves from this constant mirroring with him. We've seen seas and countries together, we've rescued less fortunate doggies together and found them families, he made us run and took us out of our comfort zone thousands of times.

He accompanied us almost everywhere making us feel at home wherever we were with him. We danced, played and swam together.

He knew how to live happily and quietly, curious to understand as much as possible of what was happening around him. He loved everything that could be loved, above all he loved people, playing ball, good food, snow, the mountains and the sea.

He knew very well what suited him, what he liked and what he didn't like and where his place was. He was careful not to disturb (especially with his big tail), had a lot of common sense and knew how to show his affection. He always showed himself as he was, and if he didn't like something or someone, he knew very well how to make himself understood.

We always found joy, peace and love in his presence. Even though we gave him everything he needed, it didn't feel like we were taking care of him, rather the other way around. In the morning he made sure to wake us up full of joy, he cheerfully stretched his spine, and his look said let's get on the carpet for morning exercise. Trust would take us for at least two long walks, one to enjoy the freshness of the morning and the other in the evening, to admire the gorgeous colours of the sunset. He never let us be upset for more than a few seconds and always reminded us to reward ourselves with a little treat. And the fact that he looked at us with such love and respect, that he trusted us so much, forced us in an irresistible way to value ourselves, to take care of ourselves for his sake too. And that mattered a lot.

He was a true example of valuing life. The way Trust lived his life was and will remain an inspiration for a life well lived, because he knew, as the great writer Mark Twain said, to:

**"Give every day the chance to become
the most beautiful day of your life."**

Trust passed away peacefully in his sleep on the very day that beloved actress and great animal lover Betty White turned 99. While we were editing this book, Betty also passed away, shortly before her 100th birthday. The fact that people all over the world considered her to have died too soon (at 100!), is the living proof of a life well lived.

"Once you've been lucky enough to share
a true love story with a golden retriever,
life and the way you see the world,
will never be the same again."

~Betty White

We always hoped that we would spend a few more beautiful summers together with Trust and that we would travel to a few more countries and a few more seas, but life happens as it happens, not as we plan... Trust now lives in the hearts of those who loved him and continues to bring smiles through the beautiful memories left behind. And in our hearts, Trust is as alive as ever.

In the end, we reproduce the beautiful words spoken from the heart by our dear friend, Viggo Johansen. He had known Trust since he was a puppy. They had a game of their own, in which they ran around and had fun together. You could see how much he loved Trust and Trust loved him. He was among the first we told that Trust had left. We have always felt him by our side. He told us sincerely: "I could cry, but when I know what a fantastic life Trust has had, I can only feel joy for everything you have lived together!"

There was so much truth in those words that we felt them like a sword that cut through the cloud of pain that had engulfed us and let the light of truth shine through. They had a great impact on us because they conveyed something true, and truth has the power to save and set us free. Trust lived a wonderful life and it's good we never forget that.

"When we lose someone we love,
we must learn not to live without them,
but to live with the love they left behind."

~ unknown author

All these years we felt how Trust's big, curious and bright eyes that constantly looked at us, were like a video camera that transmitted somewhere in the Consciousness about the life that he saw. And that made us be more careful as to how we live our time, which is limited. It was like a silent witness that conveyed to us without words:

I see you, I love you, I'm here with you.
You are never alone.

Trustisms
~ the aphorisms of Trust

We laughed and cried together, experienced the most beautiful and incredible adventures, but also some of the hardest and most painful moments. However, it was the most valuable journey during which we were enriched with many understandings, which we called Trustisms.

Trustisms are understandings that Life, in its surprising way, has revealed to us through our interaction with Trust. It's almost unbelievable how a dog can remind you what humanity really means.

He showed important and vital qualities, which we humans in our daily rush ignored until we ended up not finding them and missing them. We have come to miss living in peace, taking time to enjoy the presence of those around us and feeling **the gratitude and joy for being together on this sacred journey of Life**.

Trust spoke to us without words, in his simple and expressive way, about friendship, loyalty, respect, dignity, patience, sincerity and the courage to show yourself as you are. Nobel laureate for literature, Orhan Pamuk, said this very beautifully: "Dogs really do talk, but only for those who know how to listen."

Trust also conveyed to us how important it **is to be a calm, loving and silent presence** around someone going through difficult times.

Trustisms are understandings that become more and more precious as we manage to live by them more consistently in our daily lives. Seeing that they really work for us and contribute a lot to the way we perceive and experience life, we decided to share them. Who knows, maybe someone else will be curious to test them.

In every given moment we have
what we need for that moment.

Dogs are joyful because they don't miss
the present moment dwelling on the past
or dreaming about tomorrow.

Being yourself is enough.

Whatever you do, put all your heart in it,
otherwise it's a waste of time
and nobody has that.

Regardless of the weather
and the times we are living in,
every day is a good day for something.

Doing what you have to do and resting
are two equally important things.

Don't wait for so called
special moments to fulfil you.
The fact that you're alive is very special.

All our actions have consequences.
Move your *tail* carefully.

When you are tired you are allowed to rest,
without feeling guilty that
you have so much to do.

Respect the rhythm of life.

You have to take care of yourself first,
so you can be there for others.

Some will confuse your gentleness
with weakness. Those are not your people!

Life happens every moment,
not only in the moments we like.

Dream when you sleep,
live when you're awake.

You have to be proud of who you are,
but never conceited.

True beauty is not just about the outer aspects.
It's about the naturalness and the nobility with
which you carry the beauty into the world.

Each being sees only the reality
he can understand at that moment.

The fact that you don't bite doesn't mean you
won't get bitten sometimes.

Dog is honest.
It won't wag his tail if it doesn't like you.

Not all people will like you or you them,
and that's fine.

Do not wake those who sleep,
both literally and figuratively.

Do not measure or compare
yourself to anyone,
even if others measure themselves up to you.

We can live very well without knowing envy.

Our duty is not to please anyone,
but to keep our heart pure, warm and alive.

Even if they don't have a watch, dogs always
know the time for what is meaningful for them.
Like food or walking time.

Your actions tell everything about you.
Not your words.

You learned your lesson only when
you don't repeat the mistake.

You can be of great help by being
quiet and calm next to someone.

Dogs know to show gratitude
for what life brings to them.

In the eyes of our dogs,
we are all perfect and beautiful.

Be gentle and don't forget to include yourself.

We are. What a wonder!

We bring ourselves into the world.

Our presence in the world matters,
even when we no longer believe it!

In lovely memory

of Ecaterina Comișel, "the English teacher" who happened to be the first proofreader of this book, Romanian edition. We had just received the sample copy of the book, which we were flipping through with emotion, when we heard a soft voice from behind, asking us: 'what book are you reading?' It was the voice of our lovely neighbour. She was almost eighty years in that time. When we told her, she was so enthusiastic, asked us if she could see it and started reading from the back cover, telling us that in English, this part is called 'blurb'. There were no words for what we felt: an immense joy that for the first time our book was in someone's hands, mixed with a curiosity and impatience to receive the feedback.

The teacher had a vast linguistic experience, so her opinion mattered a lot to us. She kept us on our toes for a few moments, then smiling, she told us: 'I really like this phrase, you're right. I never thought in this way. Can I keep the book to read it?' We both breathed a sigh of relief.

The next day, early in the morning when we went for a walk with Joy, the Labrador we now have in our lives, we were greeted by her from the balcony: 'congratulations, I stayed up all night and read it, I couldn't put it down! I found out new things, which at my age happens rarely; in some places it intrigued me and the most important thing is that it amused me. You wrote like some writers!'

We were left speechless, luck with the blush on our faces, which conveyed the joy we felt. We managed to say a shy 'thank you' to which she continued: 'if you find some suggestions useful, we'll meet in the afternoon.' And since then, we kept meeting and spending great and useful time together. We went through all the text in Romanian and a large part of the text in English. The work meetings with her were fascinating, they took us like on an encyclopaedic journey. She was a kind and caring woman and a gifted teacher. We miss her radiant smile, every time when we pass by her window…

Acknowledgements

Thank you to all who trusting us and chose to open our book. We have the hope that you will find something worth it.

We thank our Romanian readers, their reviews gave us the courage to move further with this edition.

Thank you to those who have been part of Trust's wonderful life, you were our inspiration and because of you these real stories were possible.

We thank all those who listening to our stories about Trust told us that these are film material, and this prompted us to write them, so that others can enjoy it as well.

Thank you to a lifetime friend, Adi Cîmpean, who always cheering us on. The first to come in our mind when we wanted a second opinion for an English word or a saying.

Thank you to Andreia Leete who took the time to read the manuscript and make useful, fine and important suggestions.

Thank you to Sara's human, our dear friend, Anca Rugină, who read the story and gave us her valuable insights. Sara and her family loved spending time together with Trust who was so proud to walk Sara on the beach.

Grateful for Joy, our tricksy Labrador who ate our manuscript and in that way he let us know that it was a good book, especially that he had previously nibbled on a few selected works. And also because he does not mind when sometimes he is called Trust. He has shown us that if you have Trust, Joy comes too. And perhaps most importantly, that Love goes on through him…

Our warmest thanks to dear Viggo Johansen, for always being there for us when we needed him. We are deeply grateful to have such a friend that through his way of being constantly invites us to recognise what is essential in the midst of life's changes and to follow that.

Our deepest gratitude to dear Vigdis Garbarek, without whom we would have missed the chance to see life in all its splendour and wonder and also to fully understand Trust's role as the companion of our lives. The meetings we have had together over the past ten years have helped us see more clearly the difference between Life and the story we tell ourselves about life. Also inspired us in choosing the title of this book. Thank you for always being there for us, encouraging us to dare face reality with honesty and trust.

Deeply grateful to Life
for giving us its most precious gift
~ **Love** ~

Cristi & Violeta

are a married couple living in Bucharest. Cristi was born at the Black Sea Coast and Violeta in Transylvania. They graduated together from the Kutschera Institute (where they met, twelve years ago), with a master's degree in neuro-linguistic programming and they studied mind-fulness with some of the most renowned teachers. They share their passion for story-telling and for writing in a heartwarming way about what they noticed in the every day hap-penings, trying to highlight humour in various situations of everyday life. The forth-right and touching way of their writings are inspiring and invites the reader to see things from a different angle. They love to explore the world with openness and curiosity, enjoy spending time in nature and can hardly resist gastronomic temptations, *just like a Labrador* how they often joke about them selves. Insightful and hilarious, "Life happens" is their first book published in English.